Your Guide to a Strong Family

LOVING
and
CARING

~

ALWAYS
and
REGARDLESS

16,000 Strong Families Share Their Secrets

By
DR. NICK STINNETT & NANCY STINNETT

FAMILY VISION PRESS

www.familyvisionpress.com

Loving and Caring/ Always and Regardless
Copyright © 2005 by Dr. Nick Stinnett and Nancy Stinnett

All rights reserved. Printed in the United States of America.

Published by Family Vision Press
13333 Lakewood Loop
Northport, Alabama 35473
nstinne1@ches.ua.edu
www.familyvisionpress.com

Library of Congress Cataloging-in-Publication Data
Loving and Caring/ Always and Regardless /
Nick Stinnett and Nancy Stinnett

p. cm.
Includes appendices

1. Family – United States. 2. Parenting – United States.
3. Marriage – United States. 4. Communication – United States.
5. Stress Management – United States.
6. Interpersonal Relationships – United States.

ISBN 0-9744586-0-0

Printing by: Davis Printing
Graphic Design by: Carolyn Gilbert
Cover photo by: Nick Stinnett

With love we express deep

appreciation to the many strong

families around the world,

to our own families, and

to our friend and colleague,

Dr. John DeFrain,

who has for many years been a world

leader in family strengths research.

Many thanks.

Family Vision Press

is dedicated to

increasing strength and

hope in families.

CONTENTS

PART I – ALWAYS AND REGARDLESS

PART II – LOVE AND CARE FOR EACH OTHER

PART III – CREATING A STRONG FAMILY

INTRODUCTION
WHAT MAKES A FAMILY STRONG AND HEALTHY?

W here were you on September 11, 2001, when first you heard of the events in New York City, Washington, D.C. and Pennsylvania? Most likely you will always remember.

During that day and the days that followed, the news reports mentioned several calls that were made via cell phones from inside the World Trade Center Towers and the planes that crashed in Pennsylvania and into the Pentagon. In fact, most of what we know about the events on the plane over Pennsylvania is because of those calls.

What did people in those terrible circumstances – knowing they were facing death – think about? We can't know the thoughts of everyone, of course. But those who were able to call, called family and friends to say, "I don't think I'm going to make it. I love you." "I just wanted to tell you one more time that I love you. Goodbye." "Take care of yourself and the kids. I love you."

Most of us would have done the same. For most people the "bottom line" in life is this: the relationships we have with other people – our family and friends.

What's So Important about Family?

Throughout history, the state of the family has determined the state of individuals and nations. If you think that is a grandiose statement, consider the pattern seen in the rise and fall of the great societies of ancient Egypt, Greece, and Rome. When those nations were at the peak of their power and prosperity, the family was highly valued and strong. But history makes it clear that when the quality of family life deteriorated, the strength of the nation deteriorated simultaneously.

The same holds true today. We are confronted daily with evidence that the quality of family life is crucial to our happiness, emotional well-being and mental health. There isn't even a question about it any more: We know that poor relationships within the family are related to many of the problems of society.

Furthermore, many people who haven't committed terrible crimes or abused their children or spouses or otherwise contributed to the decline of society still long for greater emotional connection to family and friends. Their lives still aren't quite as satisfying as they'd like.

Good News

Don't despair. This isn't yet another book about how bad things are. This is a book of good news about how to make your family everything you want it to be!

How?

By showing you what it takes to make your family strong and healthy. You see, this book is based on nearly thirty years of worldwide research. And this research has conclusively identified six characteristics that strong families have in common and has demonstrated the power of these "secrets" to give a family strength, happiness, and fulfillment. Think about it: Six secrets to family success *exist* and are being *used successfully* by families across this great planet. But these are "open secrets" that anyone can know and use. These six characteristics are shared with you in this book so that you can adopt them into your family!

A wonderfully diverse group of more than 16,000 families contributed to the findings of this research. They came from all walks of life, all faiths, all races – some rich and some poor. They came from every state in the nation and from over twenty-five countries around the world. They included strong two parent (never divorced), strong single parent, and strong remarried families.

One of the fascinating aspects of this research is that it points to the possibility that the basic foundational qualities of emotionally healthy families – those underlying dynamics that contribute to family satisfaction and resilience – are remarkably similar from family to family and from culture to culture. Though it is undeniable that each family is unique, mounting evidence leads to the proposition that healthy families around the world may be, in essence, more similar than different.

This book, then, is a celebration of strong families and a sharing of the knowledge it takes to make your family strong. It gives you the opportunity to learn from strong families around the world as they share their secrets of success.

What Is A Strong Family?

First, what do we mean by a family? Family, of course, includes parents and children, spouses, aunts, cousins, friends, and all those other folks we acquire by birth and by living. Any definition of family, then, needs to be broad and designed to be inclusive rather than exclusive. One definition that we like is: *A family is two or more people who are committed to each other and who share intimacy, resources, decisions, and values.*

What, then, makes a family strong (healthy and happy)? Certainly it is more than being *without* problems. Strong families have troubles – just like everyone else. We could tell you about the families in Russia who face extreme economic trials or the families of Central America who live with political unrest. Or closer to home, there's the Missouri couple who lost everything in a flood except each other and the cat.

To be a strong family is not to be without challenges. It is much, much more; it is the presence of guidelines and the ability to surmount life's inevitable challenges when they arise.

Strong families are pleasant, positive places to live because members have learned some beneficial ways of treating each other. Family members can count on each other for support, love, and loyalty. They can talk to each other; they enjoy each other.

Members of strong families feel good about themselves as a family unit or team; they have a sense of belonging with each other – a sense of *we*. At the same time, no individual gets lost or smothered; each family member is encouraged to develop his or her potential.

Strong families are able to survive the crises that come their way. They unite to meet challenges; they are effective problem solvers. They pull together to pull through.

Simply put: A strong family is made up of people who love and care for each other always and regardless.

PART ONE
ALWAYS AND REGARDLESS

A strong family is made up of people who love
and care for each other always and regardless.

In spite of cultural, political, and language differences, the strong families investigated around the world are very similar. This research and the research of others who study families confirm six major characteristics of strong families.

A deep desire we all have is to experience loving and caring relationships that last and endure over time. The fulfillment of this desire is made possible by three of the six qualities that support the "always and regardless" aspect of good families. Good families endure the test of time: They can be depended upon. Certain traits help them to do so.

CHAPTER ONE
COMMITMENT

C ommitment is the bedrock on which every enduring family must be built. Commitment means that each family member knows that the others are there and always will be there and that the family is above everything else – work, recreation, other people, crises, or whatever. With commitment a family has the ability to develop the other five characteristics that make them strong and happy.

No one in a committed family lives in fear that he or she might be booted out or that some other family member will abandon them. In the atmosphere of trust and security that mutual commitment creates, every family member can survive any bad time or personal failure. They aren't afraid to expose their emotions and vulnerabilities. Neither are they afraid to love and forgive the idiosyncrasies or failures of each other.

Commitment creates the warm, loving, accepting environment in which families grow. It offers a harbor that shelters family members from the destructive forces of fear, anxiety, rejection, and loneliness.

It's no wonder that commitment serves as the basis for everything else. When family members are committed to the family unit and to each of the individuals in the family, the other key characteristics can be built on that foundation.

Although the dictionary describes commitment as a *pledge* or an *obligation*, we prefer to think of it as a *conscious decision to be dedicated to someone and/or something*. In simple terms, commitment is a promise.

PROMISE # 1:
TO THE MARRIAGE RELATIONSHIP

A number of years ago, Kathy Simon, a graduate student at the University of Nebraska, surveyed nearly four hundred experienced, successful dads from across the United States. She asked them, "What is the best gift a father can give his children?"

STOP! Before you read further, what do you think they answered most often?

• Trips to Disneyland?

•A new Mustang on a 16th birthday?

•A great college education?

•Maybe you thought more philosophically – His time? His love?

No to all of these – although they are good answers.

Kathy reports, "The best gift a father can give his children is a happy marriage." (If you're a single parent, please don't be dismayed at these words. Read Promise #2.)

Some of the men in Kathy's study were divorced and had seen the pain that marital discord and dissolution caused their children. Even so, the fathers recognized that their children's well-being was closely related to the strength of their parents' marriage. If the marriage was going poorly, to a great degree, so went the lives of the children.

Children do best in homes with happy parents who love each other and demonstrate that love in everyday commitment. Kids who see their parents loving each other feel secure in the longevity of the family. Their parents' commitment to each other also shows the parents' commitment to the children and to the family as a whole.

PUTTING IT TO WORK

Devote time and attention to making your marriage better.

Having a solid marriage means more than gritting your teeth and suffering through.

Marriage enrichment seminars offer opportunities to get to know some other couples, to learn some skills (communication, conflict resolution, coping with crises, for example), and to share relaxed recreational time.

Marriage mentoring programs match newly-married (less than seven years) couples with couples married a bit longer (seven to twenty years) and with "old" married folks (more than twenty-five years). They meet in groups of three to four couples for a meal or dessert and conversation about topics related to marriage. Everyone learns from everyone else in the group and all the couples are encouraged.

Less formally, set aside couple time periodically. Have a date: Go on a romantic picnic; rent a boat at the local marina and explore the lake; bicycle in a nearby state park. Go out of town for a weekend at a fancy hotel; lounge by the pool and dress up for dinner. Leave the kids with grandparents or a sitter. Don't talk about them. Talk about other things; flirt; hold hands.

Renew your wedding vows.

Some couples have discovered a heightened sense of commitment by renewing their wedding vows. A wedding anniversary is a good time to do this. Choose a special location – a chapel or a garden, for example. Invite a few friends to witness the event and have an informal reception afterward. Wear your wedding dress (if you still fit into it) or your veil.

PROMISE # 2:
To Be A Great Single Parent

Chuck's wife walked out one day leaving him with their two young children. She had struggled unsuccessfully with depression and drug abuse. In time, they divorced. Chuck learned to cook and to braid his daughter's hair. His parents help him with child care and emotional support while he works part time and is finishing graduate studies.

———

Elizabeth's parents divorced when she was two years old. She relates:

I don't remember much about the actual divorce. My dad has always paid child support and done other things to provide for us – even though he complains all the time about not having any money. He's not rich, but he has enough. He's a good man, just pinches those pennies! My sister and I spent weekends, summer time, and holidays with him – typical sort of visitation schedule.

Neither my mom nor dad has ever talked bad –criticized – the other. They've done a great job of continuing to be good, loving parents to me even though they haven't been married to each other for most of my life.

In an ideal world, children would live in a family with two parents who had a wonderful marriage and who loved them (and hot fudge sundaes would be diet fare, too!). In the real world, where families are torn by anger, violence, substance abuse, infidelity, and apathy – divorce sometimes happens. In some instances, such as domestic violence or child abuse, divorce may be a safety measure.

In the real world, increasing numbers of children are born to single moms (and a few are adopted by single parents). And of course, some marriages are ended by the death of a spouse.

Some of the families in the research on strong families were single-parent families. Two parents with a solid marriage are not required for a family to be healthy and happy. Obviously countless single parents are doing a great job and are to be applauded for their extraordinary efforts to rear their kids in a strong family.

PUTTING IT TO WORK

If you're not living with the father/mother of your children, make every effort to keep the co-parental relationship as good as possible.

Speak kindly (at least politely) about each other to the children. Avoid blame and criticism of each other to the children. Reduce conflict between you: Keep it between you – not in front of the children. Often this is not easy. It may require the adults to be polite and cooperative in spite of their personal anger and hurt.

Arrange and facilitate good child support, custody, and visitation arrangements.

Children benefit by a relationship with both parents if it is possible. Again, the adults involved may have to set personal anger aside to make custody and visitation arrangements that put the welfare of children first. Make child support payments on time. Provide some extra assistance with other expenses such as school fees, music lessons, or camp.

PROMISE # 3:
To Be Faithful

Tricia noticed a change in her husband during the Christmas season. He seemed overly tired – not his usual energetic self. At first she suspected a health problem and urged him to get a check-up. It was fine. Soon he was snappish as well and she thought perhaps he was troubled by something.

He was. Within a few weeks, Tricia's loving concern broke him down. He confessed that he had been having an affair with a woman at work. He told Tricia that he loved her and begged her forgiveness.

The affair had been a big mistake and it was over, he told her. He never loved Sue – never even thought he did. It all started when Sue had begun riding out to inspect construction sites with him (as a part of their work responsibilities). They enjoyed friendly conversation. Soon she was telling him about her marriage problems. He felt sorry for her and consoled her – first verbally and then with hugs. One day when she was especially sad, he kissed her and one thing led to another.

Commitment and sexual fidelity are so closely linked in most people's minds that an extramarital sexual affair is regarded as the ultimate threat to a marriage. No other enemy seems as dangerous as the "other" man or woman. No hurt seems as deep as betrayal by a husband or wife.

Because an extramarital affair poses such a potent threat, it is important that we briefly consider the dynamics involved, and more importantly, how strong families deal with affairs. The dynamics of affairs are difficult to sort out because each affair is unique. For example, some married people become involved with a stranger; others with a friend – maybe even with a spouse's best friend. Some strayers have only one affair; others are chronic philanderers. Extramarital liaisons differ in duration too – from one-night stands to long-term relationships.

There is a difference in the kind of hurt felt by those whose spouses are involved in relationship affairs and the kind of hurt felt by those whose spouses are involved in short-lived affairs. Either affair creates tremendous hurt, but greater damage is almost always experienced by those whose spouses have longer, more-involved relationship affairs.

Another dynamic also comes into play. While any infidelity is devastating, repeated instances are so ruinous that they create a scenario where it's almost impossible to salvage the marriage. In contrast, one-time "mistakes" typically can be overcome if each partner is willing to work to get past the affair.

Tricia's initial reaction was devastation, anger, and grief. She contemplated piling all his stuff into his truck and setting it on fire. Her sister advised her to get a divorce. She sought counsel from a family therapist. She cried and spied on her husband – parking outside to see if he went to lunch alone and came home immediately. She and her husband talked and talked and cried together.

Finally Tricia decided that she would not divorce him. He appeared to be truthful when he said the affair was over. She reasoned that they had both invested energy and emotion into their almost-eighteen years of marriage. The marriage had been a good one for most of that time, too. She wasn't willing to throw it away.

Tricia demanded some changes at work; her husband transferred to a different department, for example. They both visited the family counselor who helped them with the healing process. With time, they restored trust in the marriage. On their 20th anniversary they renewed their vows in a ceremony that both described as more meaningful than their "first marriage."

It may surprise you to know that for some couples who now have solid marriages, overcoming an infidelity crisis in their marriage was an important step in their long process of becoming strong. This is certainly NOT an endorsement of extramarital sex as a way of improving marriage. And none of the strong families in this study recommended anything but sexual exclusivity. On the other hand, an extramarital involvement need not automatically end a marriage.

When both parties in a marriage decide to commit themselves to each other with a commitment that surpasses their attraction to any other person or thing, they can develop a healthy, loving marriage and a healthy, loving family. Even if the commitment in a relationship has been violated, it can be restored; and when it is, the relationship can heal and become strong!

PUTTING IT TO WORK

Take certain steps to reduce the chances that your marriage will be impacted by an affair.

- **Consider the consequences.** If you had an affair, how would it affect your marriage? Even if it didn't mean a divorce, the marriage would change. What is the <u>least</u> harm that could happen? What is the <u>worst</u>? Be realistic!!
- **Be wary of rationalization.** Many affairs begin this way. "She needs my help; we need time alone to discuss things." "His wife doesn't understand him. He's so lonely. I only want to hold him and comfort him."
- **Avoid "dangerous" situations.** These are situations where opportunity is present and temptation is high: traveling together to conventions or long hours working together alone, for example.
- **Build your partner's self-esteem.** People need to feel attractive and interesting. Spouses sometimes take each other for granted and forget to be attentive.
- **Keep romance alive.** Marriages need a sense of adventure and spontaneity. Court each other, go out on dates, send flowers, write love notes, and have fun together.
- **Deepen intimacy.** True intimacy means sharing many parts of life. It is being partners, companions, best friends, and lovers. Intimacy requires lots of quality time together.

PROMISE # 4:
TO EACH FAMILY MEMBER

Commitment in strong families isn't only to the family unit or between spouses, it is also to each individual in the family. Nick explains:

I like to think of it as being 100 percent for each other. And an incident from my childhood demonstrates this kind of commitment. I was four years old, and we lived on a farm in Alabama. The house was set on a hill several yards from a busy highway. One summer morning my mother told me she was going to walk down to the mailbox, which was located just across the highway, to get the mail. She asked if I wanted to go. I was busy playing and told her no very emphatically. I watched her walk down the driveway. As she approached the mailbox, I changed my mind about going. I began to run very fast. As I ran, I yelled, "I'm coming! I'm coming!" What flashed through her mind must have been terror as she turned to see me nearing the highway: For she also saw a car — to which I was oblivious — coming at high speed. She knew in that instant that I wouldn't stop and the car wouldn't stop and I would surely be killed. She dropped the mail, raced across the path of the speeding car and scooped me up. We both fell on the shoulder of the highway. The car — which never slowed — barely missed us. My mother narrowly escaped death saving my life.

I've often thought about that incident in the years since. It was one of my favorite stories as a child; I loved to hear it told and retold. As I got older we joked about Mom moving so fast. But as you might guess, even in times when I strongly disagreed with my mother or became irritated by something she had done, I never doubted her 100 percent commitment to me.

PUTTING IT TO WORK

Read good books as a family.

Read Alex Haley's *Roots*, Louisa May Alcott's *Little Women* or *Little Men*, Lew Wallace's *Ben Hur*, or Pearl Buck's *The Good Earth* together. Or read them individually and discuss them. These stories deal with commitment in relationships and can stimulate discussion about commitment with your children. Laura Ingalls Wilder's *Little House on the Prairie* and other books are suitable for younger readers.

Rent movies (or tape TV shows) that deal with commitment in relationships or examples of good family life.

Heidi, Fiddler on the Roof, Little House on the Prairie, The Waltons, and *7th Heaven* are some examples. Watch your selections together, have popcorn or cookies, and then talk about what you've seen. What did these families do that was good? How are we like them?

PROMISE # 5:
TO PUT FIRST THINGS FIRST

WHEN WORK GETS IN THE WAY

Flashes of insight take only an instant, and I'm thankful for one I had on an airplane one afternoon. I was off on my usual business travel, which took me away from home three or four days a week. I'd left a teenager disappointed because I'd miss her dance recital. My wife felt so swamped that she'd described herself as a "single parent." I had a growing sense of alienation from my family; sometimes I missed big chunks of their lives.

Indignantly I thought, "Yeah, but they don't mind the money I make. I have work to do. It's important!" Then the flash of insight came.

What frontier was I crossing? I wasn't curing cancer or bringing world peace. My company markets a soft drink. A soft drink! Granted we sell it all over Ohio and are moving into the Pittsburgh market, but how many gallons of soft drink would I be willing to trade for my family?

I didn't quit. I enjoy sales, and it's a good job. I make good money. But I did learn to say no to some company demands. And now I plan my travels so that I have more time at home. Sometimes I take my wife or daughter along.

In a few years I'll retire, and within a few months of that, I'll be forgotten in the soft drink market.

But I'll still be a husband and a father. I'll be that until I die.

Work and the demands of work – time, attention, energy – all too often infringe on family. What do strong families do about the pressures of work on family life? Obviously, they don't quit work altogether. One thing they do is continually remind themselves that family is more important than income, career, or prestige. They find creative ways to put family first: one works part time; over-time is bypassed unless it is an emergency; or no work is brought home, for example.

Some strong families manage the pressures of work by balancing work and home. Many couples do that by sharing responsibilities for childrearing and housework more equally – even though the changes may not be smooth and easy.

Both husbands and wives in strong families are willing to change and lend a helping hand to the other. The support and aid they give each other (and to their children) are visible manifestations of their commitment to each other and to the family. A few of their comments illustrate this:

> *My husband's business is seasonal, so some periods are quite hectic for him. I try to help by mowing the lawn and doing some of the other things he normally does around the house.*

> *We were not able to make it financially any longer on the farm. So we sold everything and moved to town. My wife is teaching school to support us while I go back to college to train for another career.*

WHEN LIFE GETS HECTIC

When asked, "How do you cope with work, family, and all your other activities?" one mother responded by laughing, "Not very well!" All of us feel that way at times. The press to do many things seems to be part of modern life. Besides work, there's recreation, community activities, PTA, church, Scouts, sports leagues, volunteer work, and the list could go on.

How do we manage the busy pace of life without hurting our families? Our strong families give us the answer. Their lives get hectic and fragmented too. But they control the madness.

> *Things can creep up on you. No one would take on so many involvements all at once. But over the years, I had joined a fraternal organization, volunteered to help with my son's soccer team, begun teaching a class at church, enrolled in a class to learn how to do my own income tax returns, and begun swimming each day at the YMCA. This is all in addition to work, yard, and car care. It was too much. One week I had only one night at home. I decided that I could hire someone to do the income tax, attend every other fraternal meeting, and*

swim four days a week. If that doesn't help as much as I need, I'll let the soccer team win with me on the sidelines – just cheering.

This dad/husband was willing to examine his involvements and to make some sacrifices for his family. His actions are similar to those of the athletes who forego dessert, caffeine, and late nights to get into top physical condition or the musicians and artists who discipline themselves to invest the necessary time to refine their skills.

The strong families who mentioned cutting out activities, civic involvements, or work demands in order to enhance family life realize that it isn't enough to give family their leftover time. Leftover time isn't enough to produce successful musicians or athletes. Why expect it to produce a successful family?

We usually think of sacrifice as giving up something really important. However, this is often not the case. Sometimes, we don't even miss the things we abandon in order to make a larger investment in our families.

At the heart of sacrifice is the ability to put the best interests of someone else ahead of self – an unselfish attitude. This unselfishness is a demonstration of commitment to family.

PUTTING IT TO WORK

Have periodic family priority-setting sessions or councils.

Meet once a month, quarterly, or biannually – whichever suits your family's situation best. Discuss how "things" are going: Who's doing what; progress toward family and individual goals; any new goals; and any problems, for example.

When "too little time and too much to do" is a problem – and it typically is – have family members list and evaluate their involvements and eliminate or reduce some. (Yes, use paper and pencil for this part.) Each family member signifies his or her individual commitment by cutting outside activities so that family takes precedence.

PROMISE # 6:

TO HONESTY

During a marriage enrichment seminar, one husband talked about his wife's honesty:

> *She's like a rock in that regard. I can always count on her to tell me what she is thinking. Fortunately, her interior self is as kind as her exterior self. She somehow has managed to become a person who holds few grudges and harbors little anger and resentment. I love her for it, and I strive to be as good and kind as she is, though I slip up on occasion. She's genuine!*

When people recite the strengths of their families, it is remarkable how often honesty comes up in the discussion. Family members count on the integrity of each other, through thick and thin.

Now we are not talking about the so-called honesty that conceals criticism and that borders on verbal abuse; nor are we discounting the importance of tact or the ability to keep one's mouth shut when words will do more harm than good. We are talking about words and behaviors that are sincere, genuine, and consistently real – tempered by love and kindness.

Honesty also means an absence of exploitation or manipulative behavior. There is no ulterior motive or "flim – flam" hidden in interactions. For example, at a gathering of his extended family, he says (in the presence of several others and in a light-hearted manner), "My wife just didn't know what to bring for the potluck. She's such a terrible cook! She can ruin the best recipe. Isn't that right, sweetheart?" This exchange is a criticism veiled as humorous. Furthermore, she is pressured to "agree" or to appear overly sensitive.

Honesty in relationships allows us to trust each other, to be certain of each other.

PUTTING IT TO WORK

Examine your interactions for hidden agendas or maneuvers.

For example, are you working overtime or doing many extras at home and then using your efforts to make family feel obligated or guilty because you've worked so hard or sacrificed for them?

PROMISE # 7:
TO FAMILY TRADITIONS

Traditions in families have been described as the "we always" of family life: *We always* carve pumpkins at Halloween.   *We always* have hugs at bedtime. We always …

> *Each night when I put the baby down in his crib, I carry out a little ritual – even when he's asleep. I say, "Mama loves you. Daddy loves you. Your brother loves you. Grandmother loves you. You're a sweet, wonderful boy, and we're very glad you're with us."*

———

> *At some time during the Christmas holidays we read <u>Miracle on 34th Street.</u> We take turns reading aloud. We have popcorn, apple wedges and eggnog on that night. My grandparents started this tradition when they were newlyweds.*

———

> *I traced our family tree several years ago and I'm glad I did; but the list of names and dates wasn't very exciting to the kids. So we bought a tape recorder and asked older family members – grandparents, aunts and uncles – to record what they remember: places they lived, occupations, how they celebrated holidays. We have also begun visiting areas where the family lived. We had good luck finding farms and the old homes of grandparents and even great-grandparents. We've used vacation time to visit some of those "home counties" and poke around in courthouse records and cemeteries for traces of family.*

When strong families make traditions – whether it's always having Sunday brunch together or an annual trip to the beach – those traditions build an awareness of the unique and loving bond (commitment) of each family member to the others.

PUTTING IT TO WORK

What are the traditions in your family? Take care to continue them.

Especially safeguard them during hectic or difficult times so that they are not lost.

If you feel that your family lacks traditions, decide on some that you might like to begin. In situations where families are blending – stepfamilies or the marriage of adult children – "old" traditions may need to be adapted or "new" traditions begun.

How do you begin a tradition? First, consider your family's likes and dislikes. If everyone loves camping, then an annual campout can be fun. If, however, half the family freaks at bugs and hates sleeping bags, you'll want to consider something else – perhaps a mountain cabin. Then practice the tradition. As the TV ad says, "Just do it."

Remember that some traditions may be small things that happen every day – such as getting a hug when you head out to work or to school. Not all are elaborate or expensive events that happen once a year.

PROMISE # 8:
TO ENDURE

THE LONG HAUL

Whether you call it dependability, dedication, or bulldog determination, it is an important aspect of commitment in families. Strong families clearly reveal that commitment is for a long time. Over and over they said that they expected their families to endure.

> *We were reared to regard marriage as an until-death-do-us-part kind of arrangement. I can't say we'd never (never say never, you know) divorce, but we haven't considered it yet, and we've been married twenty-six years.*

> *My son is in his last year of high school, and I'm facing the fact that my relationship with him is about to change quite a bit. He'll be out on his own, married, and with kids in a few years. I remind him that things may be different, but I'll still be his mother. That will not change.*

> *Sometimes I think that one of my greatest assets is that I can hang in there. I've been accused of being just plain stubborn! But seriously, there have been times in life when we made it through a hard time (like when my mother-in-law was dying with cancer or when we opened our own little antique shop) in large part just because we stuck with it. And together, of course.*

A ROSE BY ANY OTHER NAME

If you've flipped through this book to find out the six secrets of strong families, you may have been surprised to discover that "love" is not listed. You may wonder why.

That's because too many of us think of love as a feeling – butterflies in your tummy, tingles in your toes, fireworks when you kiss. And of course, those are wonderful feelings! It's great when your spouse's presence makes you feel all aglow. But real life has moments when you disagree and days when the kids drive you crazy. Moods fluctuate; feelings change.

Thus, the word *commitment* is used to describe a special kind of love – a love steady and sure that isn't subject to mood swings or the passage of years or hard times. It is a love that is conscious and unconditional. Commitment-love says, "I decide and promise to love you because of who you are, not what you do or how I feel."

In the gardens of Arbor Lodge, home of J. Sterling Morton, father of Arbor Day, is a monument with a poem that follows. It sums up commitment-love quite nicely.

Time flies.

Flowers die.

New days

New ways.

Love stays.

CHAPTER TWO
SPIRITUAL WELL-BEING

A few readers will be tempted to skip this section altogether, saying, "If I want preaching – which I don't – I'll go to church" or "Don't try to cram religion down my throat!" If that's your reaction, please bear with us a while.

The strong families who have shared their secrets of success with us have come from all over the world. They represent numerous races, cultures, and faiths.

Nearly all of the members of strong families profess a belief in a higher power – God (even though their ideas of "God" are rather diverse). Most are affiliated with a group of persons who share similar beliefs – a local congregation or spiritual community.

Other persons in strong families, however, do not participate in any organized religious group. They see spirituality as an individual matter.

Because of this diversity of specific beliefs, it was amazing that the need for spirituality and a belief in a higher power was evident to all. Families all over the world, from a variety of cultures, recognized the reality of a power outside themselves.

When strong families are described as having spiritual well-being, then, we don't mean that they are religious fanatics. They do recognize that people are more than physical bodies; people also have spirit, soul, or character. They are families with a spiritual center that is vitally important in helping to hold the families together and to make them strong. Spiritual well-being brings blessings to the family that help it to endure

BLESSING # 1:
PURPOSE OR MEANING IN LIFE

I started my adult life with a bang, you might say. My parents were moderately well-to-do and gave me a good start in my own business. It flourished, and things looked rosy for ten years or so. Then the economy went sour at about the same time I had made some risky investments. One by one, those went down the tubes. In the end, we lost everything – house, cars, and the business.

My wife and I sat out by the lake one night and talked until the sun came up. I remember feeling stripped of everything – as if I'd been robbed. "Why try again?" I asked her. "We may work and work only to lose it." We struggled with that a long time and finally decided that we had been thinking wrong. We'd been so occupied with making money and the daily "busy-ness" of life that we'd allowed God and people to be crowded out of our lives.

We reminded ourselves that the purpose of life isn't to accumulate money, swimming pools, cars, and fur coats. The purpose of life is to love and honor God and to express God's love toward each other. We decided to take time to grow closer to God, to enjoy life – because it is such a precious gift, to cherish our family and friends, and to help other people.

The investments of time and effort we make in family and friends, in charitable work, and in improving ourselves can never be lost. Things in the mind and heart can't be taken away.

We did start over again and have enjoyed success. We've replaced many of the material things we lost; but most importantly, the job, the possessions, the money are no longer an end in themselves. They are a means of making life pleasant and serving God and others. If I lost them all tomorrow I'd still feel rich.

"What is life all about?" "Why am I here?"

Members of strong families ask themselves these questions – just as the rest of humanity does. And the answers come from their spiritual nature:

Life is about helping or serving others.

I'm here to rear my children and grandchildren.

I'm here to take care of my family.

Life is about making the world a better place to live.

And on and on the list could go.

PUTTING IT TO WORK

Volunteer your time and muscle and money to a cause.

You can do this as an individual or as a family unit. Most churches and communities have benevolence programs that need volunteers to do things like pack food boxes or sort clothes for distribution to needy families. Consider being a foster parent. Help at Special Olympics. Organize or help at a free or low-cost medical/dental/vision clinic. Join in the collection of relief supplies for the victims of natural disasters. Find where Habitat for Humanity is building a house in your community.

Join a discussion group (or form one with your friends).

Consider religious topics, value-related matters, or philosophical issues. Current events in the news are always a source of topics.

BLESSING # 2:
GUIDELINES FOR DAILY LIVING

Spiritual well-being is a very personal, practical, day-to-day matter in strong families. Religion is neither superficial ritual nor highly theoretical theology.

We are committed to a spiritual lifestyle that is livable. Maybe that's because we're practical people by nature. The beauty is that so many spiritual teachings are very practical if you only give them a chance. Take, for example, the teaching that when we are angry we are not to sin. We aren't told not to get angry; that's unrealistic. We are told to manage the anger, and that's excellent advice. Temper tantrums, unresolved resentment, and uncontrolled conflict can be very damaging to the individual and to relationships.

———

Our family has certain values: honesty, responsibility, and tolerance, to name a few. But we have to practice those in everyday life. I can't talk about honesty and cheat on my income tax return. I can't yell at the kids about being responsible and turn my back on a neighbor who needs help. I'd know I was a hypocrite, and so would the kids and everyone else.

———

The most recent conversation in our house has been about our television-watching habits. We – as a family – are evaluating how much we watch and what we watch. If a half-minute commercial can convince us to buy a certain toothpaste or cereal, doesn't it seem logical that a whole show can convince us to buy certain habits? We don't condone excessive drinking, marital infidelity, smoking, or violence. What influence does it have on our lives to watch all that on TV? I don't mean to get on a soapbox here, but this is a good example of how we try to apply our spiritual values to real life.

Members of strong families believe that there are moral truths – "rights" and "wrongs" – and values that guide daily living. When people abide by their values, their lives have direction. And daily living – including relating to family members, friends, the boss, and others – is better because of their positive values and practices.

PUTTING IT TO WORK

Identify weaknesses and strengths.

Begin with three of your personal weaknesses (lack of patience, poor temper control, worrying too much, for example). Decide how to improve in these areas, and then put your plan to work. Select three of your strengths (neighborliness, compassion, honesty, etc.) and make a conscious effort to develop these traits more fully.

Now apply this exercise to the family unit. What are three areas of spiritual well-being where the family needs to devote some attention (attend worship service more often, have more patience with each other, be kinder to each other)? Then discuss three areas of spiritual strength in the family (hospitality, benevolence to the needy, etc).

Cherish your spiritual heritage.

Religious history and heritage provide guidelines for living, good models for character development, and a sense of belonging. Read (individually and as a family) stories about spiritual leaders, heroes, and heroines. Also select stories that are inspirational and that teach timeless truths about living the best way.

BLESSING # 3:
FREEDOM AND PEACE

I was having one of those particularly difficult times. Everything seemed to be going wrong at work; my folks weren't doing well health-wise. A routine physical had turned up a lump in my breast. Naturally all I could imagine was cancer.

Partly to distract myself, I went to a shopping center and was meandering through a gift shop when I saw a plaque that said:

> *Sometimes God stills the storm*
> *To calm his frightened child.*
> *Sometimes he lets the storm rage*
> *And calms his child instead.*

I immediately bought it and went home. Two possibilities awaited me – either my troubles would clear up or God would strengthen and quiet me to meet them. Either way I didn't have to worry or be afraid.

———

Small groups of people meet in this room twice a week. The church-basement room has two sofas and some chairs around a small table. A basket with assorted hard candies sits beside the coffee pot; boxes of tissues are scattered about. The sign outside the door reads, "Al-Anon Family Group T TH 6:30pm."

People come here because they have a family member who is addicted to alcohol or drugs. They and their families are dealing with legal and financial difficulties, shame, fear for the health and safety of the addict, hurt, and disappointment. They share experiences, comfort, and encouragement; they seek understanding and insight to change their attitudes.

The groups that meet here in this room begin and end each meeting with a recitation of the Serenity Prayer. This prayer helps to reshape and guide the thinking of the folks who come here.

God grant me the serenity
To accept the things I cannot change,
Courage to change the things I can,
And wisdom to know the difference.

Freedom from worry, anger, anxiety, and fear is not the only freedom that spiritual well-being brings to strong families. Many report a freeing from guilt and low self-esteem.

I believe that I will be forgiven if I can forgive others. It's similar to the law of physics about every action having an equal reaction. If I forgive I am forgiven. So I don't have to carry around a load of guilt.

I like the analogy of a human body in thinking about the importance of each person. Each of us has talents and skills. My talent may be less than yours or greater than someone else's. It doesn't matter. We each have a contribution to make. The whole body can't be "eyes" – some parts have to be "ears" or "feet" – and it takes all the parts working together to make the body complete.

PUTTING IT TO WORK

Set aside fifteen to thirty minutes each day for meditation and prayer.

Take a walk to get away from phones and interruptions. Take in the beauty of nature – the dawn song of the birds, the wildflowers along the highway, or the cool blue of the lake. Listen to inspirational music as you drive. Sing along! Read the Bible or other inspirational works.

BLESSING # 4:

A POSITIVE, CONFIDENT OUTLOOK

Meet Bob and Vernita Garriott, two of the most positive, confident people we know:

>They met at a small college in Oklahoma, courted and decided to marry – very much like many other couples. Unlike most, they decided (after long and prayerful consideration) NOT to have biological children. Why? Vernita is legally blind due to a hereditary trait. Bob was born with only a left arm. They didn't want to pass along any genetic liabilities: They decided to adopt instead.
>
>So they finished undergraduate degrees in education and sociology. And when they felt ready for parenthood, they applied to adopt a child. Immediately they ran into barriers. "How will you be able to feed a baby?" they asked Vernita. "What if you get your hands dirty changing a dirty diaper?" Vernita answered that she thought washing hands after changing a diaper was a good idea – even for people with excellent vision. They were not impressed.
>
>Their efforts to adopt were stalled, delayed, or diverted for almost two years. During that time civil rights legislation was enacted and eventually they were offered a child with special needs. A charming little guy – Kristian – needed a home. He had been born without feet or fingers; the development of his limbs had stopped at that point. He also had a cleft palate, was missing 80 percent of his tongue, and had cranial nerve damage, causing his face to be partially paralyzed.
>
>Bob and Vernita spent much time in prayer, considering whether they should adopt Kris. They had felt guided by God to adopt children. Perhaps they were supposed to parent children with special needs. After all, their personal experience and professional training (by this time, Bob had completed his master's degree in vocational rehabilitation) made them uniquely qualified. Years later, Vernita would laugh, "They didn't think I could see well enough to feed a normal baby, so they gave me one who required special bottles and

nipples because of his cleft palate. Figure that one out!"

Kris grew and flourished – even with numerous surgeries. He was an active preschooler when Ricky joined the family. Ricky had several strokes during his birth, resulting in permanent brain damage. Ricky also added another dimension to their family. He is of African-American descent. "We were criticized by folks at church and within our family," Vernita explains. "They didn't think we should cross racial lines. And they argued that we wouldn't be able to help Ricky much because he was severely retarded."

But the Garriotts remained confident that God's plan for them was to help children who were at risk or who were difficult to love. They adopted Kevin, a troubled teen who had come to them in foster care – because he asked them. Eventually, the Garriotts came in contact with Holt International Children's Services, a Christian agency devoted to helping homeless children around the world. Through Holt, they learned about a young man in the Philippines who needed a home, and so sixteen-year old Domingo came into the family. Not long after that, they adopted Becky, a young girl who had been in foster care most of her fourteen years. Her birth mother was suspected of having thrown her from a moving car when she was eighteen months old. As a result of her injuries, Becky has some mild cognitive difficulties and is prone to seizures. "But Becky has the distinction of being our only daughter," observes Vernita. When Becky made some mistakes in judgment (as an older teen), Bob and Vernita adopted her baby, Nikki Joe.

Not long after that, Holt International asked Bob and Vernita if they would consider taking other children. Bob and Vernita were approaching the age limit for adoptive parents, but Holt ministries sought them out because they were the best couple for the job. And so Victor, a tiny, blind baby from Guatemala; Kyle, a street orphan from Brazil; and Mark, a severely burned child from Thailand, joined their family. "Things had come full circle," Vernita said. "In the beginning, we were told we weren't capable of caring for children, and now we were being sought out."

Their story doesn't end there. Kris has completed his undergraduate degree in recreational therapy and works in a related field.

Kevin and Domingo live and work far from home, now; but they both visit when they can – and call often. Becky lives with her cat in her own apartment in the same town as Bob and Vernita. Nikki Joe, now "Nik," and Kyle will soon finish high school. Both have part-time jobs and are interested in cars and girls. Victor, who beat the odds just by living, is an avid fan of car racing.

The successes and victories of the Garriott family are many. They have also had difficult and sad times. Mark was unable to adapt to life in the U.S. When he was old enough, Bob and Vernita helped him return to Thailand. They no longer hear from him. The family has had other challenges, too: troubles at school; scrapes with the police (try rearing that many boys without any!); criticism from people who don't agree with them; finding money to feed, house, and transport the crew (a van with a wheelchair lift for Victor, for example); and securing medical and social services for all their special needs.

As Bob and Vernita – and the children – grow older, a main concern is arranging for the ones who will continue to need special care. Ricky already lives in a facility for men like himself. He shares a cottage with several others and enjoys jobs of delivering the laundry and shredding paper at attorneys' offices. "He could have worked for Enron," notes Vernita with a laugh. He is content and well-cared for. Victor will live with one of his brothers – likely Kris. Nik understands his "extra" responsibility to Becky. All in all, everyone will be cared for.

You may ask, "How do they manage?" They have a deep and abiding conviction that the work they do is of great value. They've had help from many friends. And Bob and Vernita are people whose steadfast faith in God has guided them in their choices and spurred them on when things got tough. Their spiritual center has kept them confident and positive.

BLESSING # 5:

SUPPORT FROM LIKE-MINDED PEOPLE

They moved to town in July and settled into their new home and community. In December they made a trip to visit his ailing mother. They were out of town when the F – 4 tornado went through their neighborhood: A dozen people died; many were hurt; more than 125 homes were destroyed.

They left immediately to make the five-hour trip back. Their neighborhood looked like a war zone. Trees were down; entire homes were gone – only the concrete slabs remained. It was bitterly cold and rainy. Their house was damaged beyond repair, but what was left was a busy place. People from church were already there – working. Some ladies had taken wet clothing and linens to launder out the mud. Other belongings were being cleaned, dried, and packed. Debris was being stacked.

At the next worship services, they spoke of their gratitude to the people of the church. He said, "When we drove up and saw you working there, we were deeply touched. You haven't known us long enough to love us this way, but I'm glad you do."'

In addition to the support found in our physical families, the fellowship and support from people in an extended spiritual family can be invaluable. Other strong family members told us of support and aid from people of their spiritual families during illnesses, births of babies, deaths, and natural disasters such as fires or floods. And even during good times, the contact with like-minded people is a source of encouragement, a reminder of values, and a model for conduct.

BLESSING # 6:
SHARED BELIEFS

Members of strong families recognize that squabbling over theological details or matters of opinion brings heartache and animosity – not the hope, joy, and comfort that spirituality should bring. Disagreement that grows to dissension destroys the atmosphere of spiritual well-being in a family. And yet, folks in strong families may disagree. So, what do they do then?

Many have realized the need to reduce or defuse destructive dissension. One way to reduce disagreement is to seek to understand each other's point of view. Be open to the idea of studying about the issue. Ask questions and then listen to the answers. Focus on shared beliefs.

> *My wife and I were reared in different faiths – Jewish and Christian. We have each learned about the beliefs of the other. We do have large amounts in common even though there are some obvious differences. We are teaching our children about both faiths. Right now they are young and think this is OK. December is really neat as far as they are concerned. With Hanukah and Christmas, they have presents, parties, and goodies for a whole month! When they're adults, they'll choose for themselves.*

Respect for the person who disagrees is crucial to reducing dissension. In areas where family members cannot agree, strong families often decide to "agree to disagree." Both recognize and acknowledge that they see things differently. They do not get caught up in judging each other, criticizing, or character assassination.

Religious leaders and counselors hear terrible stories of how bickering over spiritual questions has become a nightmare in a family. Because spiritual well-being is so crucial to family strength, each person should be encouraged to search out and find his or her own faith. Then, seek to understand others and to treat them with respect. Finally be ready to forgive others and yourself for being human.

BLESSING # 7:

ACCESS TO A POWER
GREATER THAN THEMSELVES

We join in family prayer each evening. We pray for each other, for guidance with our decisions, and for help with our problems. This puts us on a higher level of thinking and opens new dimensions for us. Our family becomes a circle of power; prayer energizes us.

———

Welcome to the Tuesday evening meeting of the Al-Anon Family Group. Tonight the group reads the Twelve Steps – as is their custom. Steps 1, 2, and 3 say:

"1. We admitted we were powerless over alcohol – that our lives had become unmanageable.

"2. Came to believe that a Power greater than ourselves could restore us to sanity.

"3. Made a decision to turn our wills and our lives over to the care of God as we understood Him."

In the discussion that follows, one woman shares that there is a shortened version of the first three steps that goes:

"I can't. . .God can. . .I think I'll let Him."

And an even shorter version that says:

"Let go and let God."

For most of the strong families, the central aspect of their spiritual well-being is a belief in a power greater than themselves. They rely on God (even though the specific understandings of God vary) as a source of wisdom, love, and power.

Others view the source of power greater than themselves more impersonally – as universal laws that govern all actions. People reap what they sow: If you're cruel to others, you'll eventually be treated the same way, for example.

Or they may conceptualize power as coming from the combined wisdom, will, and goodness of the group – the idea that two or more people working together can accomplish more than would be possible based on their individual skills. The interaction between them results in the total accomplishment being more than the sum of the parts.

Regardless, they feel – as stated in the Al-Anon literature – that they must have help beyond their own abilities to deal with life most successfully. The trials of life are bearable and surmountable because of the spiritual resources they tap.

PUTTING IT TO WORK

Find or create sayings or slogans that encourage and inspire you.

Put them on index cards in places where you will see them: on the kitchen window, the refrigerator, the dash of your car, the bathroom mirror. Find posters or pictures with beautiful scenes and inspirational sayings or scriptures.

Listen to, sing, or play music that inspires you.

CHAPTER THREE
COPING ABILITY: STRESS AND CRISES

STRESS

You might have seen the poster of a zebra whose rear haunch and leg stripes have come unraveled. As the zebra stands with its stripes curled around its feet like ribbons, the caption notes, "It must be STRESS."

We've all felt like that zebra – as if our stripes are falling off. It could be because traffic is extra heavy, the tub won't drain (again!), or a check has bounced. Happy events also bring stress: moving to a new home or town; giving a holiday party; or bringing home a new baby, for example. Stress comes in many shapes and sizes – and on a daily basis.

Stress is not new, but our understanding of it has grown in recent years. Our ancestor who encountered a bear while foraging for food experienced stress. Adrenaline flooded his body, his blood pressure surged, and his heart beat faster. He was ready to run faster or fight better as a result. Those same reactions take place in our bodies today when we are stuck in a traffic jam or the boss snarls or a deadline draws near. Unfortunately, those situations don't require fight or flight, and so we experience the strong physical and emotional reactions to stress without an effective way of releasing them.

After months or years of such distress, we feel the effects. Medical science has much evidence that the accumulated effects of stress are important factors in heart disease, angina, arrhythmia, hypertension, migraine headaches, ulcers, diabetes, and many other diseases.

The bad news is that stress can kill us; it can diminish the quality of life in our families; and we can't get away from it. The good news is that we don't have to succumb to stress – we can take action to manage it. Strong families have discovered some tactics for dealing with stress that have proved successful for them.

TACTIC # 1:
KEEP THINGS IN PERSPECTIVE

Everyone has difficult times. Who doesn't have days when you get a parking ticket, the boss is cross, traffic jams, the neighbor's dog gets in your trash cans, it rains, and the washing machine blows up? I try to remember that I have plenty of company in misery. That helps me get through.

———

One day I was feeling really pressed and depressed. We had guests coming for dinner, the house was messy, and I resented having to cook and clean. As I washed dishes, I suddenly thought of a young woman we knew. She was gravely ill and too weak to get out of bed. We knew she didn't have long to live. What would Annette give to have this "awful" day of mine? How happy she'd be to be able to be up cooking and cleaning or any number of ordinary things.

Knowing we aren't alone or unique gives us courage and a little more enthusiasm for tackling our troubles head-on. Sometimes, thinking of others helps us realize that our problems aren't so big.

PUTTING IT TO WORK

Learn to recognize the little bugs.

An old adage says, "It's not the great storm that destroys the giant oak tree – it's the little bugs!" It's ironic that we, too, can weather the great crises in life and then allow trifling irritations to destroy our happiness and health.

Learn to recognize the stressors that really are insignificant or minor. Some are best overlooked and forgotten. The driver who honks and whizzes past may be late for something VERY important. The neighbor who doesn't return your wave may not have seen you.

What about those trivialities that you can't ignore – a mate who slurps coffee or who teases in a way that hurts your feelings? Members of strong families offer suggestions:

Iron it out as soon as possible. Be nice. Say, "It really drives me nuts when you crack your knuckles. I know it isn't a big thing; you're a fine person with few flaws." You'll both have a laugh and clear it up.

———

Don't let resentment build up. Don't pile misunderstanding and hurt on top of misunderstanding and hurt. Get it out in the open. Ask the person who hurt your feelings what was meant. You may discover you misunderstood the action or words. If not, forgive them and go on. Life is too short.

TACTIC # 2:
LET IT GO

I used to worry a lot; in my business it's easy to do. It got to the point where it was about to break me. Then a very important thing happened to me, and I don't know exactly how: I finally realized deep within myself that it was not possible for me to control every little aspect of my life and the lives of others – as I had been trying to do.

I decided that I should do the best I could and then let go. I had to trust more in other people and in life.

———

I used to go through two routines: what if and if only.

"What if it (rains, snows, is too hot, doesn't rain)?" "What if it won't work?" "What if they hate me?"

"If only I hadn't said ...." "If only I had done it differently." "If only I were ...."

And on and on. I was always miserable.

A friend suggested that I write down a list of worries each week. Then I could sketch out what to do about each. I liked that approach, but the real shock came when I looked back at my list several months later. Many were things in the past I couldn't change, and some were things in the present I couldn't control, like whether it rained. I decided I'm too smart to waste so much time needlessly.

Worry has been likened to a rocking chair: You make a lot of motion but don't go anywhere. Worry depletes energy, keeps us fearful, and interferes with our effective functioning.

PUTTING IT TO WORK

Use music to help you to release worries and anxieties.

Listen to calm, soothing music to help you relax, meditate, or fall asleep. Spend time playing music that quiets your fears and worries. Sing songs or hymns that reassure you.

TACTIC # 3:
FOCUS ON SOMETHING BIGGER THAN SELF

Sometimes in the scrambled schedule of life, I get to feeling that the time I spend with my sons could better be spent on work. And then I remind myself that the budget request or schedule of who works when or the productivity report will affect life for a few days or weeks. I have to do it and it's important, but my job as father is most important. If I'm a good father to my sons, they'll likely be good parents too. Someday – after I'm gone, and certainly after those reports have rotted – a grandchild or great-grandchild will have a good father because I was a good father. It's a chain reaction.

Having a mission or goal – being caught up in something larger than ourselves gives us security, confidence, and serenity to deal with the stresses of our daily lives.

PUTTING IT TO WORK

Keep the big picture in mind.
    See those PTA meetings as improving the school; see your volunteer hours as easing someone's misery; see driving the carpool as communication time with your kids.

TACTIC # 4:

LAUGH

We try to treat things seriously that need it and poke fun at the rest. We often ask ourselves, "Will this be funny later?" and a good many are. I'll give you an example:

We headed out to the company potluck dinner one evening in a bit of a fluster because we were about five minutes late and my husband was supposed to give the invocation. At the trunk, juggling keys and a casserole, he tipped the dish and spilled hot casserole on his hand and trousers. He dropped the dish onto the lawn (killing the grass in that spot!) and raced back inside to change clothes.

We dashed off and were halfway there when a police officer pulled us over. We had missed a new no-left-turn sign at an intersection. Of course, the officer wanted to see my husband's license, and you know where his wallet was? Right! At home in the other trousers. There we sat explaining spilled casseroles and changed clothes to the officer. She let us go with a warning. No one would have made up a story like ours.

We arrived at the dinner and my husband said, "I'm sorry we're late, but I am very thankful just to be here. Let me tell you why ...." His humor changed a blood-pressure-raising series of incidents into a good story.

Many people in strong families prescribed humor as an antidote for stress. "Learn to laugh at the crazy things that happen and at yourself," they suggested.

PUTTING IT TO WORK

Cultivate your sense of humor.

Collect Ogden Nash poems or books by your favorite writer of humor. Make a scrapbook of cartoons you especially enjoy. Buy a Dilbert or Far Side calendar. Use a VCR to make a collection of your favorite comedy series. *I Love Lucy, Andy Griffith, Frasier,* and *The Simpsons* are examples. Rent or buy favorite funny movies.

Gentle, kind humor – humor that is not at anyone's expense – is the most refreshing. Humor that "puts down", humiliates, embarrasses, or hurts increases stress.

TACTIC # 5:
REDUCE THE LOAD

Consider the following story. As you read, you may think it's an exaggeration, but it's not.

The editor of one of the largest newspapers in the nation was very successful in his career. Active in community programs and various philanthropic endeavors, he almost never had an evening at home. He was always involved in a meeting or project. All of his projects were worthy, but all of them together were simply too much. A sad thing happened.. He caught the flu because his body's resistance was low from overwork.

He died.

People can literally die from a load so heavy that it overwhelms the mind, the emotions, and the body. In such a weakened state, a person becomes more susceptible to viruses, bacteria, and the like.

In a similar way, families that are burdened by too many involvements are weakened in their resistance to negative influences and encounters. Strong families deal with the problem of too many involvements by scratching some activities off their lists, by clearing their calendars, by learning to say, "No."

Another way strong families deal with too much to do – too many demands – is to simplify what must be done.

> *We simplified meal preparation by cooking most of the week's meals on Saturday. We grill a couple chickens (while we cook our Saturday burgers), fix a large casserole, and a big pot of soup or chili. This gives us something to take for our lunches at work. When we come home in the evenings, all we have to do is warm up something and add a salad or dessert. This has saved us considerable time, aggravation, and money.*

PUTTING IT TO WORK

Nurture each other.

Give a kind word and a helping hand to a family member who is overwhelmed: Do a chore that he/she usually does; remind him/her of accomplishments, strengths, and resources.

Simplify.

In any area of life, think of ways to make tasks simpler and easier. For example, for lower maintenance, replace annuals in your flower beds with perennials or shrubs. Try gravel/mulch and a few plantings in large pots for color. Hang unsoiled clothes worn to work or to a meeting to wear a second or third time before laundering. Shop in the smaller, independent grocery where it is easier to park, find things, and check out.

TACTIC # 6:
Refresh and Restore

We like to take what we call "aimless" trips about twice a year. We decide on a general destination not too far away. Then we set out and go as we please. We take state and county roads and drive leisurely. We explore little museums, quaint shops, and roadside markets. We stop early to enjoy a swim at the motel before dinner.

Quilting is my refreshment. I can spend the evening quilting or looking through patterns and fabric, and the tension just goes away. I'll be excited about finishing my current project or looking forward to starting a new pattern.

Try hiking or sailing or biking all day and feel that "good" tired feeling of physical fatigue. So much of our fatigue these days is mental that it actually refreshes us to tire the body and let the mind rest.

I go to the gym – regularly – to "de – stress" myself. Usually I work out with weights and then stationary bike or swim. Swimming is the best tension reliever for me.

My mom and dad have a very special dog who comforts and cheers them with his unconditional love. They'd tell you that he thinks he is a short, four-legged person. He looks like a Bichon Friese or a cocker/poodle mix. No one knows for sure; he was a stray. When mom has something to eat or drink that he wants he gets a perky look on his face and wags his tail stub. She understands and shares with him. He likes cherry tomatoes, cold coffee with milk, peppermint patties, and ice cubes – and pretty much everything else that she eats.

And he can liven up a dreary evening by starting a game: He gets one of his many stuffed toys and drops it at someone's feet. If it's you, you have to grab it quickly or he will. Then the toy is tossed down the hall or hidden from him (behind someone's back, for exam-

ple). He's pretty smart and is hard to fool. Soon everyone will be laughing and having a good time. By the way, he knows the family members most likely to play and brings a toy promptly when they come by. My sister comes from out of town to visit about once a month and she always brings him a new toy. So when she comes in and sets down her purse and bags, he starts sticking his nose in the bags, looking for his present. That's part of why he has a huge basket of toys. He's spoiled!

We all need to restore our minds, spirits, and bodies. Members of strong families find rest in activities that are pleasant. They mention being involved in outside activities, exercise, and pets as powerful antidotes to stress.

PUTTING IT TO WORK

Select a hobby that refreshes you.
Pick something that contrasts with what you do all day at work. If you work at a desk, get out in the garden, for example.

Commit to an exercise program.
Walking is generally safe, effective, and free. Play tennis, swim, ride a bicycle, or go canoeing with loved ones on the weekend. Check with your doctor if you've been inactive, if you have health problems, or have any concerns about increasing your activity level.

CRISES

Paul Harvey often points out on his news broadcasts that "you can run but you can't hide." Some things are inescapable. Daily life brings the strain of irritations, frustrations, demands, and hurts. Living brings change: a new baby, a new job, moving to another town, a wedding, children moving out of the home, retirement.

But sometimes life brings major upheavals: serious illness, death, unemployment, fire, divorce, flood, marital infidelity, earthquake, or bankruptcy, to name a few. What about these more disruptive events—these crises?

In the Chinese system of writing which uses pictographs to convey meaning, the symbol for the word crisis is a composite of two other symbols: the symbol for danger and the symbol for opportunity. The implication is clear: While crises undoubtedly bring difficulty and sometimes danger, when viewed positively and creatively, they can be opportunities for personal and family growth.

The family strengths research has identified some strategies used by healthy families in crises situations. These strategies help their families to make it through — to endure.

STRATEGY # 1:
SEE THE ROSES AMONG THE THORNS

Larry was in his mid 30's with a truly good life – loving wife and three beautiful kids, robust health, nice home, good job he loved – when a freak accident in a friendly basketball game changed his life forever. The accident didn't seem serious at the time: He and another player jumped for the ball, tangled up and came down hard – the other man's elbow digging into Larry's lower back.

Larry had experienced athletic injuries before so at first the pain didn't worry him. But the pain became worse – excruciating – accompanied by dizziness, weakness, and nausea. Months of medical tests and hospitalizations finally yielded an answer: a rare disease of the pancreas triggered by the blow to his back.

And then came the really bad news: the condition was disabling and practically always terminal inside of two years. They traveled to the Mayo Clinic to find the best medical care for this disease. The latest treatment, including removal of the pancreas, offered only a slightly better prognosis – maybe only two or three years to live. They decided to try.

Life has been a struggle for them ever since. He had a number of surgeries - almost dying numerous times – and hospitalized repeatedly for infections, pneumonia, liver failure, kidney failure, and heart attacks. Not a year passed without at least one hospital stay. The removal of his diseased pancreas induced diabetes so that several times daily injections of insulin were necessary.

Unable to work, he was declared disabled. Anne went back to work and soon was working at two jobs (one full and one part time) to pay bills. They moved closer to parents and siblings so that family could help them more easily.

Over the years Larry set goals for himself: to live to see the family settled in their new home; to see the kids graduate high school; to see the kids graduate college. Early in 2002, he suffered a massive heart attack. Doctors told him there was nothing they could do to help. His body was too debilitated to endure any medications or treatment.

Even though he was very frail, he was able to go home again. He told Anne that he wasn't afraid – he always felt okay as long as she was with him. His goal this time was their 40th anniversary.

He collapsed and died on November 20, 2002 – at home with Anne and Jennifer and Brent, their children who live nearby. He was buried on their 39th anniversary.

It has been almost thirty years since Larry played that fateful basketball game. No one would have been surprised if he and Anne had divorced and the children had run wild!

Instead the family has endured; he and Anne enjoyed a close, solid marriage; and the children are fine young adults. A number of factors have contributed to their ability to cope with this crisis, of course, including faith in God and help from their church family, extended family and friends.

They, too, have been remarkable in being able to see something positive in the situation and to focus on that. Here are some examples:

As a six-year-old, Brent had said that he was happy that his dad was home a lot. Larry saw that as an opportunity to feel good about and take advantage of the time he had with his children. He was an excellent father – a companion, a friend, a teacher, a confidant to his children.

They have always been touched by the kindness and generosity of the people who have helped them. They saw having to move closer to parents and siblings as an opportunity to strengthen family ties. The children's lives have been richer for knowing their grandparents, aunts, uncles and cousins.

A few years ago, with the children grown and out of college, Anne was able to quit her part-time job. She was so thrilled to be working only one job! Although, of course, she reminded everyone, she was thankful that she had been able to find two jobs that fit together and that she'd had the stamina to work them when the family needed the income.

Now please don't get the wrong idea here. No one's suggesting that we should be naïve fools merrily dancing a jig while the world goes up in flames. Nor are people in strong families unrealistic Pollyannas who are never knocked down by tragedy. They cry, get angry, feel hurt, and are depressed. But they are not overwhelmed by crisis and tragedy—partly because they manage to see some good in bad situations. Their ability to do this helps them maintain a more balanced perspective; it prevents them from becoming so depressed and despondent that they cannot function; it gives them hope.

There's a poster that sums up what we've been talking about. It says:

Roses have thorns or
Thorns have roses.
How do you see life?

PUTTING IT TO WORK

Cultivate the ability to see something good in a bad situation.

Practice on news stories ("Yes, that family's house blew away in the tornado, but they're all O.K.") or events in your past ("It was difficult when grandma was so ill and lived with us but we learned a lot of our family's history from her stories.")

STRATEGY # 2:
PULL TOGETHER

A while ago we were moving as a result of a job transfer. My sister came to help us pack. We couldn't have made it without her. If she hadn't come, I'd still be there packing boxes.

———

My mother was in reasonably good health — for a person of her age — until about seven months before her death. Then a number of conditions seemed to get worse rather quickly. She was physically weak and somewhat disoriented. We made the decision to stay with her in her home (rather than bringing her into ours) because she was more comfortable with her own stuff — and more familiar surroundings were less disorienting.

My wife and I swapped out staying nights with her so that the other could go home to our pre-teen son and to take care of things that needed done there. I stayed with her during the week because I had greater flexibility with my work schedule. A neighbor lady checked on Mom around noon. My wife got off from her job in the early afternoon and would come out to cook dinner, help Mom bathe, do laundry, etc. Usually we all ate dinner with Mom. After dinner, our son would help Grandmother do her physical therapy exercises. She always cooperated better with him than anyone else!

Sometimes she'd be confused and think our boys were her sons. When we'd tell her differently, she was always so pleased, "Oh! I have two grandsons! They're such nice boys, too."

It was a challenge at times. Mom needed help with bill-paying and taking her medications and everything. We neglected housekeeping at our home; we didn't like being separated at night. But we were able to make Mom's last months as pleasant as possible. She'd always feared having to go to a nursing home. She didn't have to do that; she died peacefully during an afternoon nap — in her own bed with her kitty curled up beside her.

Members of strong families unite to face the challenges of a crisis.

They ask, "What can I do?" Sometimes the task is enormous. Nobody can do it alone. Strong family members focus on the small things they can do as individuals. No individual feels total responsibility for the problem. Nobody carries the load alone. They shoulder it together.

PUTTING IT TO WORK

Consider your family as a team.

See yourselves as on the same side and "pulling together to pull through." What needs to be done in this crisis? Who can do the myriad tasks? Find tasks for everyone in the family. Focus on getting the family through – not on who usually does certain chores or who's working harder (or longer or better) or who's getting all the attention (praise).

STRATEGY # 3:
GO GET HELP

My wife was cleaning out closets and passing on outgrown clothes to the Goodwill box when she found a packet of marijuana and a pipe in our teen daughter's closet. We were horrified and frightened. As soon as we collected our wits, we realized we weren't equipped to handle this alone.

We talked with our family attorney, and she gave us a copy of our state's laws about drug possession. We talked with a drug rehabilitation counselor who gave us information about symptoms of addiction; he recommended two or three courses of treatment, depending on how serious our daughter's involvement was.

We had done our homework when we confronted our daughter a few days later. We had solid information about the legal and physical danger she was in. We didn't have any trouble conveying our deep concerns for her, and I think she responded better than she would have to our initial shock and fear.

———

Three friends were particularly helpful to me following the death of my wife. One lady came to the house immediately; she tidied up the living room and cleaned the refrigerator because she knew people would be coming to visit and bringing food. Then she fixed the guest room because she knew some relatives from out of town would be coming. She stayed at the house all day taking calls, keeping a record of who brought what so I could write thank-you notes later. She made coffee for the friends who dropped by to pay their respects. I was in no shape to handle all that plus the funeral arrangements.

Her husband picked up my relatives at the airport and later drove them to the funeral home. They both provided long-term support by visiting me, having me in their home, and showing they were concerned.

The third friend is an older lady, a widow. She went with me to make funeral arrangements and to select a cemetery lot. She, too, was there when I needed her for years after my wife's death.

Family members – spouses, children, parents, siblings – provide much of the help that a family needs to make it through a crisis. Fortunately, most families don't have to make it alone. And strong families are smart enough to seek out valuable support from others – their church or synagogue, friends, neighbors, and professionals.

PUTTING IT TO WORK

Check out the resources in your community.
Browse the telephone book for your community (or nearest large community). Most have community information. You may be surprised at the services available: mental health services; alcohol or drug abuse treatment; daycare for adults with memory disorders; financial and legal counsel; low-rent housing; Wheels to Work (low-cost transportation); hospice; shelters for victims of domestic violence; and child-abuse prevention and intervention, to name a few. There are also support groups for many circumstances: head injuries; Alzheimer's; bereavement; divorce; breastfeeding; HIV/AIDS; multiples (twins, triplets, etc.); depression; stroke; cancer; and juvenile diabetes – again to list only a few. Some are free; many have very reasonable fees.

STRATEGY # 4:
USE SPIRITUAL RESOURCES

A few years ago, we were living in a large urban area. It was not a good place to rear our children. The lifestyle was very materialistic and hectic; it was too crowded. My husband's job, though it carried a high salary was very stressful and not satisfying. It left him with too little time for the family. In short, we were miserable.

We prayed about this for some time, and we had many serious conversations about what we could do. Finally, we came to the decision that we would leave. That may not sound earth shaking, except that we made that decision without knowing where we would go or if we could find a job somewhere else. We asked God to guide and help us, and we had faith that he would. It may sound strange, but we did not worry about it.

About one week after we made that decision, a job offer came. It was a good offer, the kind of work my husband wanted, and in our number-one choice of places to live. And my husband hadn't even applied for it – didn't realize the opening was there. The company representative who called him said they were hoping he would be interested in the job but didn't know if they could lure him away from where he was. (Little did they know!)

We put our house on the market and it sold ten days later. We located a truck rental company that had a special offer that was about half of what others were charging. A minister friend drove two thousand miles to help us move. He said that all ministers know how to pack and move. We couldn't have done it without him.

In two months' time, we made our decision to leave, had a job offer, sold our house, packed the truck and left for our new home and life. We know that only God could have put all these things in place. It wasn't luck, and it wasn't circumstance. It was God. We continue to marvel at how it all happened.

In times of crises, spiritual beliefs provide a philosophy of life, perspective, hope, and comfort. It is not surprising, then, that strong families draw on spiritual resources in times of crises, just as they draw on the physical resources of energy and muscle and the emotional resources of family commitment and concern.

STRATEGY # 5:
Open Channels of Communication

Our son was in the reserves and was deployed during the Gulf War. We, naturally, were concerned for his safety even though his job was support services rather than combat. I began having terrifying dreams. First, I dreamed someone phoned to tell us he'd been killed. A few nights later the dream went further – we were told about his death and went to the airport to claim his body. Next time, we planned a funeral – picking out a favorite hymn of his.

I was so frightened by the dreams that it was hard to talk about them. But I did confide in my husband. He suggested that my dreams were not a prophesy – after all, I hadn't had prophetic dreams before (Thank goodness!). Instead the dreams were my way of expressing my very worst fears.

As we talked, we also realized that our son would come back changed as a result of his experiences. My dreams could mean that our son's childhood and innocence would "die." Even if he came home without a scratch, he would still have changed forever.

After we explained the dreams to ourselves, they ended. And our son did come home safely.

———

As the time of our youngest daughter's wedding approached, I called a family council. Things were out of control. Weddings have a way of growing – more guests, more food, more flowers, more money! We just couldn't afford the size this one was gaining. And I was very nervous about getting all the arrangements made; I was swamped.

Our daughter – the bride-to-be – was relieved to simplify the wedding. We decided to have a less elaborate reception to reduce costs considerably. My husband suggested letting his mother do the flowers. She's done flower arranging for years as a hobby and is quite talented. He also volunteered to line up the photographer and musicians.

Both my husband and daughter were willing to help. They

hadn't realized how near an anxiety attack I was. We all felt better to get our plan of attack formulated.

One benefit of opening communication channels is that problem solving is made easier. Another valuable benefit of open communication is that it allows family members to express feelings freely. Crises are times of change and uncertainty; people caught up in them may feel loss, anger, fear, anxiety, and guilt. Being able to express these feelings is a step toward surviving the crisis.

STRATEGY # 6:
GO WITH THE FLOW

We had thought of retirement as a reward for years of hard work. All the hoopla leads up to retirement. And then you wake up one morning wondering, "Now what?"

It didn't take Roger long to catch up on sleeping late and watching television sports. Soon, he was hanging around watching me do housework. Then he began offering advice, and that was too much for me! I seemed to spend all day puttering around and getting very little done. We were both feeling aimless.

It took some time, but we worked out a style of living that suits us. For one thing, we follow a general schedule. We are not fanatic clock watchers, but we have breakfast around eight and do house and yard chores until lunchtime. We work together on the chores – Roger especially likes to cook. One day a week we go to town: to the bank, post office, grocery, and such.

Afternoons are varied. I volunteer at the hospital some and take a craft class. Roger has become active in county and state politics; he had a wonderful time working for his favorite candidates during the last elections. In slack times, he enjoys his coin and knife collections.

We visit friends at least one evening a week for cards or board games. Roger and I have been able to travel more. We took an extended trip to Australia to visit one of my elderly aunts and her children. We hadn't seen them in many years, and it was wonderful.

We had to decide how to structure our time. We had to adapt to more free time and more time together. We changed the way we divided household chores. If we hadn't been able to make those changes, we'd have been pretty miserable.

A final characteristic of strong families that allows them to weather the storms of life is their adaptability or flexibility. A proverb tells of the mighty oak, so tall and firm, that breaks in the strong wind while the fragile-looking reeds bend to the ground but do not snap. Good families tend to be like the reeds. They bend, they change, they adapt, and when the storm is over, they're still intact.

PART TWO
LOVE AND CARE
FOR EACH OTHER

*A strong family is made up of people who love and
care for each other always and regardless.*

In Part One, we presented the three characteristics of strong
families that seem most supportive of their endurance.
Commitment, spiritual well-being, and the ability to cope
with stress and crises all work together to give strong families "staying power."

But strong families don't just stay together because everyone
has a high tolerance for misery! They are pleasant, affec-
tion-filled, warm, and friendly places to live. Three other
traits help to make them so.

CHAPTER FOUR
POSITIVE COMMUNICATION AND CONFLICT RESOLUTION

That strong families have good communication patterns and skills came as no surprise. Countless research studies from very diverse fields have revealed effective communication as a factor in establishing and maintaining good relationships – at work and school, or among neighbors, friends, and family.

The experiences of living and "common sense" testify to the truth of this as well. In fact, good communication is so very important that it has been called the lifeblood of relationships.

Good communication patterns and skills help to make a strong family a place where people love and care for each other. This happens in several ways.

First, good communication builds belonging. No one wants to feel all alone in the world. We all want and need to feel a connection to others. Effective communication ensures that the commitment, love, affection, closeness, and regard that family members feel for each other are expressed.

In order to achieve the intimacy (the belonging and closeness) that they long for, people must share many aspects of their lives (dreams, goals, interests, values, etc.) and they must know each other well – not just superficially. This kind of sharing is possible only through good communication practices.

I found in my husband someone with whom I could share my thoughts, ambitions, dreams, and fears. I truly feel that we are two who have become one.

———

My parents always have time to listen to my problems and concerns. I know they'll have time for me no matter what. They're on my side.

Second, good communication promotes good mental health. Having the opportunity and ability to express negative emotions instead of having to suppress them prevents a building up of anger to the point of bitterness or rage, for example. Sharing ideas and opinions promotes seeing things from different perspectives; people can, thus, gain wisdom and balance.

The acceptance felt in true, interactive communication gives each family member a positive sense of self and self-worth. Each person listens and is listened to. Love is shared in words and in the demonstration of respect and acceptance. The resulting stable sense of self-worth is conducive to mental and emotional health.

Finally, good communication skills are helpful in very practical ways. The simple exchange of information in an efficient way helps to make daily living easier.

Then, too, strong families face the same problems as everyone else: They overdraw at the bank, the car breaks down, the teenagers sneak beer, grandpa has to come to live with them – you name it! Good communication helps ease daily frustration levels by increasing the family's effectiveness in solving problems.

Marriage and family therapists not only pinpoint a lack of communication as a source of family unhappiness, they also point out that bad communication causes unhappiness. The good news is that positive, effective communication skills can be learned and most are not difficult.

SKILL # 1:
TAKE ENOUGH TIME

A man stood silently with his son, daughter-in-law, and three grandchildren looking over the rim of the Grand Canyon of the Colorado River in Arizona. Instead of being lost in the beauty of the hues and shadows, he found himself thinking about the evolution of his family – his marriage, the birth of his children, and now the growth and development of his grandchildren. Finally his thoughts turned to the sight before them. He marveled at the incredible beauty of this national treasure and the countless years required to form it. He whispered thoughtfully, "Good things take time."

Indeed they do. And good communication takes time: Time to gather our thoughts and to express them; time to listen; time to talk about the mundane and trivial; time to talk about happy events and special times; time to talk about problems and worries.

PUTTING IT TO WORK

Make a time for family communication.
    While much communication in strong families is spontaneous – while they're doing chores or driving to school or watching TV – some families plan times for family conversation. Husband and wife may get up early enough to have coffee and conversation before the work day begins. Other families plan special times such as family night or family councils, to gather together to share happy times, plans, problems, and concerns.

Designate a mealtime as a time for sharing.
    Plan for the whole family to be together; share events of the day at dinner or plans for the day at breakfast. Avoid disciplining or inflammatory issues or hurtful topics. Keep the mood pleasant. Talk about ideas, too. Don't just gossip! Ask the kids, "What do you think about …?"

SKILL # 2:

LISTEN

The story is told that one of Abraham Lincoln's most valued advisors was a longtime friend. During times of hard decisions, Lincoln would summon his friend to Washington. And the friend would come by train for many hours to aid his friend, his country, his president.

As they spent time together, Lincoln would speak his concerns, his woes, his burdens, his options. And his friend would listen. Just listen. No advice or suggestions. No, "If I were you, I'd ...." After a few days, the friend would return home and Lincoln would arrive at decisions.

Good communication involves two steps: talking and listening. Listening allows us to understand others – to know what is in their hearts and minds. It also conveys powerful messages of respect and caring.

PUTTING IT TO WORK

Practice being an "active listener."

Active listeners listen not only to the words being spoken, but also to facial expressions, body posture, and voice tone. They listen for the feelings behind the words.

Active listeners also give responses that indicate their attention (a nod, or "okay," or "go on," for example) and that encourages the speaker to go on. When Junior comes in complaining that his math teacher hates him, an active-listener parent will note his feelings (discouragement, perhaps) and will respond, "Sounds like you're a little down about this teacher or math. Tell me about it." Junior is encouraged to keep talking.

In contrast, if the parent responds, "Stop complaining about your teachers. That isn't polite," Junior is likely going to retreat to his room and to discouragement. Communication was closed down.

SKILL # 3:
CHECK THE MEANING

One evening my husband and I were at a banquet and were sitting across the table from each other. As we enjoyed the meal and conversation with the other folks at the table, I looked up at him just as he casually wiped the side of his mouth with one finger and smiled at me. I assumed I must have sauce or crumbs on my mouth so I wiped my mouth – casually, of course – and smiled at him. He picked up his napkin, wiped vigorously, and smiled. I wiped a larger area of my face and smiled. This went on for a while before we figured out that neither of us had crumbs or sauce on us. I had misread a stray gesture of his.

Inaccurate interpretations of messages – verbal and nonverbal – happen very easily. Sometimes they are funny; sometimes they lead to serious misunderstanding and conflict. A usually-pleasant husband who is snappish and sulky may appear to be angry at his wife. If she responds with harsh words and sulks, they may soon be in a serious conflict. If instead, she asks, "You seem a bit grumpy tonight. Are you angry at me or is something else bothering you?" she may discover that he is feeling frustrated by a budget cut at work.

Vigilance in clarifying fuzzy or distorted messages helps strong families avoid two common communication pitfalls: indirect communication and mind reading.

My wife's family uses a good deal of indirect messages, and they understand each other. My family has always been pretty direct, so you can imagine the interesting misunderstandings Sue and I had until we figured this out. She'd say, "Are there any good movies downtown?" and she'd mean, "I'd like to go to a movie." I would answer the question she asked by telling her what was playing. Then I'd be surprised when she got angry or sulked. Eventually we caught on to this pattern. Now she tries to say, "I'd like to ..." instead of hinting, and I'm better about checking to be sure I understand what she really means.

Mind readers assume they know what others are thinking but don't bother to check it out. James and Debbie talk about their experience:

> *"The clearest example was over the issue of visiting my parents,"* James said. *"Debbie hadn't had much of a chance to get to know them before we married, so I assumed she wouldn't want to visit them. I'd fly out to Arizona to visit periodically, but wouldn't ask her to go."*
>
> *"Meanwhile,"* injects Debbie, *"I jumped to the conclusion that Jim had some dark, ugly reason for not wanting me along. First I thought he was ashamed of me. Then I decided he must have an old girlfriend back home. I'd fret whenever he left but never asked why he didn't want me along."*
>
> James continued, *"I stupidly assumed that her not asking to go was proof of her lack of interest. Finally my folks came here for my graduation. They enjoyed Debbie so much they said, 'You should come to visit with James.' That caused me and Debbie to discover how dumb our assumptions had been."*

PUTTING IT TO WORK

Take a hard look at your communication habits.

Are you guilty of mind reading or indirect communication? Make a concerted effort to send clearer, less fuzzy messages.

Learn, too, to ask questions. "This is what I think you said. Am I right?" "Can you explain? I'm not sure I understand."

SKILL # 4:
GET INSIDE THE OTHER PERSON'S WORLD

Early in our marriage, financial hardship forced us to move close to my in-laws. We didn't have to share a house, but we parked a mobile home on their farm. I soon learned a lot about my parents-in-law, but more important, I learned a lot about my husband from them.

One area of misunderstanding cleared up when I noted how Hank's mom keeps house. He and I had fought over housekeeping — I'd fuss that our place was messy; he'd say it was comfortable. When I got it cleaned to suit me, he felt it was too sterile. One day it dawned on me that Hank's folks are more relaxed about housekeeping. They're clean — don't get me wrong — but they like to have books and magazines handy. She always has needlework materials out on the table or scattered about the living room. And we do have different taste in decorating. I prefer simple, uncluttered designs, neutral colors, few decorations. Hank grew up with wallpaper designs, ornate furniture, and much more bric-a-brac. We've compromised on this one. And that compromise was made easier by understanding each other's point of view.

We each live in our own unique world. No one sees life exactly the same way you do. The way you look at a certain situation depends on past experiences you have had, the values in which you believe, and your personality characteristics. This means that when two people disagree on an issue, it is not always because one person is right and the other is wrong. It is more likely due to the fact that the two people come from different worlds, with different perspectives.

People who are most adept in communication have the ability to get inside another's world and to see things from that person's point of view. Social scientists call this empathy.

SKILL # 5:

UNDERSTAND IT'S A MAN – WOMAN THING!

I was so upset by something my husband did. I called him and was telling him that I'd had car trouble. I'd been behind the high school stadium on Elm Drive when the car started making a weird, chuggy noise and stalled out. I couldn't get it to start and was afraid somebody was going to rear-end it. Traffic is heavy on that street. I got out and went to that convenience store to use the phone – which was out of order. Then, I told him, I had to go to the Laundromat across the street and a lady there loaned me her cell phone. I called the garage and they'd towed the car and …. At that point he just blurted out, "What is wrong with the car and how much is this going to cost?!"

I just started to cry – it hurt my feelings so bad.

Most women readers are agreeing with her. He was an insensitive cad. How could he not be concerned about her harrowing experience with the car, traffic, phones; or how she felt about it all.

Men, on the other hand, are perplexed by her reaction. He just wanted the "bottom line" – so he could get about the business of getting the car fixed. He didn't want or need all those details.

The communication differences between men and women are interesting, amusing, and frustrating. The example above highlights some of them: Women tend to talk more than men, give more details in general, and share openly about themselves. They are more adept at starting and carrying on conversation. They interpret nonverbal messages more accurately. And they tune in to people's feelings more often.

In contrast, men are more apt to be silent types – less communicative and less likely to share about themselves. Men also want to get to the "bottom line" – the most important part of the conversation quickly. They are more interested in facts than in feelings.

PUTTING IT TO WORK

Be sensitive to the communication differences in men and women.

Remember they can be sources of confusion and conflict. Understand and minimize them as much as possible. This willingness to accommodate each other sends important messages of respect and commitment.

SKILL # 6:
KEEP THE MONSTERS IN THE LATE-NIGHT MOVIES

Remember when you were a kid and you played the monster game with your friends? Someone would yell, "Here comes the green monster!!" Everybody would scream and run. The monster game was a little scary and fun.

Adults also play a "here comes the monster" game, but the adult version isn't any fun. It creates anxiety, destroys good communication, and ruins relationships.

Eileen is a good woman at heart; she is intelligent, educated, and competent in many areas. Psychological abuse as a child left her feeling inadequate and inferior. Unfortunately she tries so hard to mask these feelings that she gives the impression that she is expert about everything. If someone asks a question, she rolls her eyes and sighs as if to say, "How dumb!" Her response may begin, "Now let me see if I can explain this in really simple terms."

———

I have an aunt who comes to visit about once a year. She's a dear woman and has many good qualities, but she always makes me feel as if I am being measured. She isn't openly critical, but I can tell she's comparing my job, my housekeeping, my children, and my life to what someone else has and does. I don't guess she realizes how much she threatens my self-esteem.

Eileen and the aunt are guilty of two communication monsters: acting superior and evaluating. Other communication monsters need to be locked up as well. These are intimidation, criticism, and sarcasm. Family members can intimidate each other in several ways – throwing a temper tantrum, engaging in actual physical abuse (or threatening it), ridiculing, threatening to leave, or becoming very cold and sullen.

Criticism and sarcasm sometimes wear disguises. Criticism can hide behind the ploy, "I'm just trying to help you improve. This is *constructive criticism*." Or it may sneak in with praise – as in, "You made a B on that test. Wow! Just think what you could do if you tried harder."

Some people think of sarcasm as sharp-edged humor or biting wit. In truth, sarcasm is veiled anger and hostility.

Over time, the recipients of any of the communication monsters dread interaction. Who wants to feel evaluated, intimidated, ridiculed, inferior, stupid, or humiliated?

NO ONE!

PUTTING IT TO WORK

Take a hard, fearless look at your habits.

Are you harboring a communication monster? Seek to understand why. Are you like Eileen and overcompensating for feelings of inferiority? Maybe you don't trust others to do the right thing unless you control them by fear. Perhaps you have picked up some bad habits. Then practice more effective ways of communication.

SKILL # 7:
KEEP IT HONEST

The communication patterns in strong families are characterized by honesty and openness. People say what they mean and mean what they say. But honesty is more than not lying.

> *We became aware this summer of a bad habit our daughter had picked up. She was exaggerating her weaknesses (for lack of a better word) in order to get people to do things for her. I think it began when she broke her ankle and discovered how nice it was to be waited on. Then we noticed she was "no good at math," so big brother was helping her by figuring her paper route bills. Or her ankle "hurt too much" to help with chores. Or she "had a headache" and couldn't go somewhere with us. We were able to correct her tactics by refusing to do things she could do herself.*

Members of strong families don't resort to bullying, outwitting, blaming, dominating, or controlling. They don't play on dependency; they aren't silent, long-suffering martyrs who create guilt. All those methods of manipulating others lead to dishonesty and shallowness in relationships.

Strong families also maintain a balance of honesty and kindness. They aren't apt to let Sis go out in a dress and hairdo that look ridiculous just because they don't want to offend her. On the other hand, they won't use one mistake in her judgment as an excuse to blast her. They'll use an approach that is positive, nonjudgmental, and non-hurtful.

PUTTING IT TO WORK

Keep it positive.
     Communication that is honest will naturally include some complaints, grievances, and disagreements. Remember to air your honest appreciation, validation, joys, agreements, support, and pleasures as well. In fact, in happy marriages and families positive communication happens much more often than negative.

Conflict Resolution

Without fail, whenever we talk about strong families, someone asks if they ever argue. Yes, they do! And there are good reasons why. Jake, a retired tailor with a good measure of wisdom, put it this way: "If you didn't care about somebody, you wouldn't get mad!" For example, a wife might get angry with her husband for driving too fast because she doesn't want him to get killed.

Another reason for conflict in strong families is this: They are real people in a real world. They disagree with each other; they make mistakes; they get fatigued and stressed; problems arise. Again, it is not the lack of conflict that sets strong families apart; it's the way they deal with it: When conflict arises, they are creative and caring.

Conflict can be resolved or at least ended in a number of ways – some of which are more satisfying than others. One way that conflict is ended is when someone in the family pulls rank on others, overpowers them, and wins the argument. This is basically a "because-I'm-bigger (more powerful)-than-you" approach. While every family on earth probably adopts this approach on occasion, its overuse can be a mistake. The problem is that when someone "wins" an argument, someone else "loses." The relationship suffers, and in the long run, they both (all) "lose."

Withdrawal is another problematic way of dealing with conflict. Somebody backs off, leaves the room, or uses the silent treatment – basically saying, "I quit."

Strong family members regularly use one of two classic, positive approaches to conflict resolution. Either they work together to come to a reasonable agreement that benefits everyone (consensus). Or they split the difference in a conflict – each one "gives" some (compromise). Several principles guide their conflict negotiations.

PRINCIPLE # 1:
Don't Gunnysack

A gunnysack is a big burlap sack used by shipping companies and farmers. Gunnysacks are strong and deep to hold large amounts of produce or other material.

We can gunnysack emotional stuff, too: resentments, hurts, and anger at injustices. Even though the bag is heavy to carry around, at strategic times (as in the heat of conflict), we reach in and pull out a grievance to throw at our opponent.

Members of strong families are more likely to resolve conflicts as they emerge – rather than storing them away to use as weapons later.

It bothers both of us to be at odds with each other. As a result, we deal with sore spots as quickly as possible. Sometimes we have to wait awhile – say until we get home from work or until we calm down a bit. But we deal with them as soon as possible rather than letting them get bigger overnight.

An added benefit of dealing with problems as they arise is that the families are more apt to be dealing with one problem at a time. Paula, from Virginia, provides some ideas about why this is a good rule to follow.

After several hair-curling arguments that started with the overextended budget and went to dirty socks stuffed under the bed to hair in the sink to both sets of in-laws to where to vacation, we wised up. How could anybody sort out all those things? If we could put socks, hair, in-laws, and vacations on hold, we could concentrate on the budget. We could handle one problem; that's manageable. Five problems at once are overwhelming.

PRINCIPLE # 2:
BE SPECIFIC

For a long time I was angry at my wife because I thought she was spending money too freely. I'd complain that she was spending too much. She'd say she couldn't cut corners any more than she was.

Finally, during one fight, she said, "Just tell me how to spend less."

"Well," I said, "You do a good job on groceries, and you don't splurge on gifts or things for yourself – but you could spend a lot less on clothes for the children."

Suddenly it hit me: That's what was really bothering me. She suggested that she could choose less expensive shops for the kid's clothes – especially play clothes.

It was rather funny. When I could narrow it down to my specific gripe, she and I could deal with it.

Strong family members have a greater track record of successes in solving problems because a specific complaint is easier to treat. "You never talk to me" is harder to manage than "I wish we could have thirty minutes each evening without TV, the kids, or the paper."

PRINCIPLE # 3:
BECOME ALLIES

It would be silly to get caught up in personal attacks when we fight. All that does is hurt feelings and fan the fires. We try to see ourselves as being on the same side – as a team. The problem is the enemy. We're fighting it – not each other.

Probably the approach of strong families that spares them the most grief in conflict situations is that of attacking the problem rather than each other. Members of strong families use good problem-solving techniques to attack the problem they're facing.

Here are some tips for effective problem solving:

- Pick the right time (as soon as possible; when there are few distractions; no one is too hungry or tired)

- Respect each other's right to disagree or differ

- Practice all your best communication skills

- Identify the specific problem as clearly as possible

- Share feelings about the problem

- List all the ways to solve the problem even if some seem silly or totally unreasonable

- Evaluate the potential solutions to choose the one that seems best for everyone

PRINCIPLE # 4:
BAN THE BOMBS

A spouse or children can be devastated in innumerable ways. We think of these implements of destruction as "bombs." They're the weapons you hold on to for that last-ditch effort. Usually you're going down fast or are consumed by anger, and so you vent all your wrath. Members of strong families have declared a freeze on such deadly weapons.

> *I know more about my husband and children than anyone else does. I know their fears, their vulnerabilities. I have power to hurt them.*
>
> *So why don't I pull out all the stops and say those dreadful things that would allow me to "win"? Because that is too high a price to pay for winning the battle. Generals make that mistake sometimes. My son is a World War II buff, and I've heard him remark several times, "So-and so won this battle, but the casualties were terribly high. They won, but it cost too much."*
>
> *I feel it would be a serious violation of the trust we have in each other to use our knowledge, or closeness, as weapons. Even when I get very angry, I keep sight of that.*

> ———

> *When I was a teenager, I read a poem about a beautiful, crystal vase. Two people took the vase off the mantle and held it between them, admiring its beauty. Then, one of them was careless and the vase slipped to the floor – shattering into a million pieces. The poem went on, likening friendship to the vase. Just as carelessness can cause a beautiful vase to be destroyed – beyond repair—so too, a friendship (or any relationship) can be damaged beyond repair by carelessness. We should always be aware that we can say things or do things that will shatter a relationship forever.*

To ban the bombs requires discipline to resist the urge to lash out or strike back – especially when you're hurt. It helps to keep a vision of your commitment to your spouse and children. Don't drop (or throw down) that vase.

PRINCIPLE # 5:
AVOID ESCALATING THE CONFLICT

Charles and Debbie had been married about ten months when she became annoyed at his habit of dropping his dirty clothes wherever he took them off. She tried to talk with him about it; he promised to change, but soon went back to old ways. This time when she reminded him, he made humorous remarks about the "dirty socks and pants gremlin" living in their home.

Debbie found no humor in this approach, but decided to try a similar tactic. She made pointed remarks about "slobs" and "lazy bums." In response, Charles observed that some people were just "rigid and bossy." Each day became a contest to see who could get in the most cutting remarks. Charles also began to notice that Debbie was rigid about other things, too. She liked to have dinner at about the same time each day and liked to plan if they were taking a weekend trip, for example. Likewise, she noticed that he was sloppy in other areas, too. He left projects on his workbench from one weekend to the next, for example. They began to disagree more often over more issues.

Debbie next refused to do any laundry for Charles any more and began stepping on clothing left on the floor. Charles, in turn, began to leave everything – dirty dishes, soda cans, newspapers, junk mail – wherever he finished with it.

Family therapists have developed a model of conflict that describes how folks can get caught in a whirlwind of conflict. Usually when conflict starts, the family members are focused on solving the problem. Emotions are under control and resolution is often achieved.

Sometimes, family members don't use their best communication or problem-solving skills or they get focused on the conflict itself. Now their energies are spent on winning the battle and they begin to outwit and belittle each other. Their hopes of resolution grow dimmer.

As personal attacks grow more vicious, the focus shifts to hurting each other. Real issues are lost in the battle; any hope of true problem solving is gone.

LEVEL	FOCUS OR AIM	FEELINGS	CHANCE OF CONFLICT RESOLUTION
One	Solve our problem	Optimistic and cooperative	Good
Two	Win the battle	Competitive	Not good but still possible
Three	Hurt each other	Angry and distant	Next to none

PUTTING IT TO WORK

Learn to de-escalate conflict.

In any conflict situation, keep aware of where you are in this model. Are you focused on solving the problem or have you begun to belittle the ideas of your opponent? Are you convinced that your opponent is all wrong or to blame? Are you caught up in name-calling, sarcasm, or pushing and hitting?

Make a conscious, disciplined effort to move back to Level One. "We're getting off course here. Let's get back to solving this problem. Remember we're on the same side."

PRINCIPLE # 6:
OPEN UP UNDERSTANDING

Silly as it sounds, we had major, ugly fights over Christmas and birthday presents. I had begun to dread any gift-giving occasion because it always ended in a big mess. Instead of being happy, we'd be mad and hurt and yelling. I'd be crying.

Things went like this. One birthday, I gave him some accessories – specialty lens and such – for his camera. He enjoys photography and is good at it. I also gave him some nice shirts for work because he'd lost some weight and needed them. He was visibly disappointed – scarcely looked at any of it. I didn't understand and was hurt.

On my birthday, he gave me an expensive, dressy watch. And I tried to be excited, but I kept thinking that we really couldn't afford it. So he was bewildered by my reaction and offended.

We did this kind of scene too many times. It seemed like the harder I tried, the more miserably I failed. He'd say, "You never get me anything nice." And I'd think, "Why doesn't he listen to me when I ask him not to buy extravagant gifts for me."

We finally analyzed – through a series of difficult discussions – what was going on. Our ideas of the "good" gift are very different. We both grew up in families that celebrated holidays and birthdays with decorations, special foods, and gifts. However the nature of gifts was different.

In his family, gifts were personal items, very nice, and usually a bit expensive – even when money was tight. They would economize on groceries or household goods, but not gifts.

In my family, gifts were also personal in nature – meaning something you knew the person wanted or needed, but could be practical, as clothes or shoes for work. We all collect something – chickens, cats, owls, etc. – so a unique or funny addition for a collection was considered a real "find." Since gifts didn't have to be costly, finding an almost-antique owl cookie jar in a thrift shop was a good gift (with a story).

Naturally after we married we each bought gifts as we had always done. And so our problem developed. Now that we understand each other better, we do better on gifts. For example, now I'd pick an expensive fragrance or a silk shirt for him. He's listened to me, too.

As is clear from this example, sometimes conflict can't be resolved until people achieve an understanding of each other – beyond words. Clarifying the meaning of messages is an effective communication skill. Sometimes it requires knowing the person well enough to know the hidden or deeper messages of words and actions.

CHAPTER FIVE
APPRECIATION AND AFFECTION

Years ago, when we began analyzing the data from the questionnaires and interviews from strong families, we anticipated some of the findings – commitment and good communication, for example. But this characteristic surprised us: Over and over the importance of appreciation and affection was mentioned. In addition, on seeing them interact (during interviews) and from the tone of written comments, we were struck by this – these folks genuinely like each other!

Yes, that sounds like a no-brainer. Too simplistic. Too obvious. It has been observed that the profound is a truth simply stated so that people react, "Oh! Of course."

Appreciation is deeply and fundamentally important to our welfare as humans. In families where people love and care for each other, they recognize the very important need that people have to be appreciated.

Think about this – why do we do so many of the things we do – work overtime, bake cookies, or clean out the garage? Having some extra money or a craving for chocolate chip cookies or a sense of duty doesn't fully explain it. We also want spouses and children to see what we do for them. We want to be valued for who we are and what we do.

Valued!

One wife said of her husband:

> *Very few days go by that he doesn't say something like, "You look really nice today" or "The house is so clean and comfortable; it's a real pleasure to be home."*

He also is sending a powerful message, "You are a person of worth and dignity. I am aware of your positive qualities. I affirm who you are and what you do." Although unspoken, this message comes through loud and clear. It enhances her feelings about herself (self-esteem).

Strong families demonstrate that appreciation and affection help family members flourish as each person's self-esteem is boosted. As a pebble dropped in a pond causes ripples all around, so pebbles of appreciation cause ripples that carry into other facets of life. The family becomes a pleasant place to be, and the environment of love makes everything better. Members of strong families share simple but powerful secrets to nurture appreciation and affection.

SECRET # 1:
DIG FOR DIAMONDS

South African diamond miners spend their working lives sifting through thousands of tons of rock and dirt looking for a few tiny diamonds. They know that what they're going to find in those mountains of dirt will more than compensate for all their efforts. Too often in unhappy family relationships, people do just the opposite. They sweep aside piles of diamonds, eagerly searching for dirt.

My husband is the classic "absent-minded professor" type who tends to forget birthdays and such. But there are other ways he shows he loves me. Last week, he saw kiefels [a kind of Croatian or Czech roll] in a Czech bakery and bought them for me because he knows how much I like them – and how hard they are to find. It made me remember again that when he forgets, it isn't because he doesn't love me.

Psychologists talk about self-fulfilling prophecies. This is a fancy way of saying that you pretty much get what you're looking for in life. If you choose to follow a dismal path, you'll have your unhappy dreams come true time and time again. If you search for the bad in members of your family, you'll find that, too, and have a miserable home life. But here's better news: If you look for the good in your family, you'll certainly find it and have a happy family life.

We fell into a trap early in our marriage – partly because of some couples we saw socially. They considered themselves to be very sophisticated, and nothing or no one quite measured up to their standards. One particular couple delighted in acid sarcasm – especially with each other.

We didn't realize how we were being affected until we left town for a three-week vacation. Soon, we felt relaxed and happy – and assumed it was the trip that had made us feel better. We came back to town feeling good, went to a party at our friends' house and came home in a depression. We were puzzled.

The next day we sat down to figure out what was going on. The sarcasm, fault-finding, and belittling were rubbing off on us. It had been a subtle process, but we had begun to see things in a negative way. It was affecting our marriage, too.

We decided to stop. Our first step was to find some new couples to socialize with. We also worked on our attitudes. We chose to accent the positive.

Now when my husband comes home, he says, "Wow! You've been busy with the boys today, got your hair cut and did the marketing." He doesn't even mention the weedy garden. And when he comes in disappointed over a sale he missed, I remind him of the three he made last week. We have conditioned ourselves to look at what we have, what we have completed, and what we are rather than what we lack, what isn't done, and what we can't be.

PUTTING IT TO WORK

Try reframing the situation.

This technique involves mental gymnastics. Many faults we see in ourselves and others are really positive qualities carried to an extreme. For example, the spouse who is stingy is really only a thrifty person in the extreme. Is your child loud and out of control, or enthusiastic? Granted, the enthusiasm may need some curbing and the tightwad may need to loosen the grip on the dollar. The point is that we view that person differently when we see the core of good. Select two or three traits of your spouse and/or children that annoy you or that are negative. Redefine them – reframe them – in positive terms. Here are a few examples to get you started.

Spendthrift; Wastes money	versus	Generous
Talks too much; Chatters	versus	Likes to share
Domineering; Bossy	versus	Shows leadership
Always into things; Messy	versus	Curious
Won't follow rules; Messy	versus	Creative
Nitpicking	versus	Attentive to detail
Meddlesome; Interfering	versus	Interested; Concerned

SECRET # 2:
BE TRUTHFUL

There's nothing wrong with rhinestones – in your jewelry. When you're digging for diamonds in your family members, only the real stuff will do, however.

———

Now, if I told my husband he is a wonderful mechanic, he'd know I was lying. But he is a wonderful dad to our sons. He spends hours with them. They go to all the construction sites to watch the cranes and bulldozers. Not all dads are like that.

———

I hate to hear people being phony in talking with children. I believe in praising mine, but I give them credit for some brains, too. I don't say, "You jump higher than anyone" to my six-year-old. She knows better. I say, "You can jump so high. You're doing good."

———

At first, some people are skeptical of my expressions of appreciation. I can tell they're wondering what I'm after. But with time, I think my sincerity becomes apparent because I'm careful not to use false flattery. If I don't mean it, I don't say it.

Members of strong families realize that it isn't necessary to be insincere in expressing appreciation, because each person has many good qualities and accomplishments. They believe that if someone makes us feel good we should let them know.

PUTTING IT TO WORK

Write down ten things you like about each member of your family.

(Five will do if you can't come up with ten – or if you have a large family.) Be specific. Say, "I like the sparkle in your eyes" rather than "You're nice-looking." No mixed messages, such as "I like you, even though you're a butterball." Don't put all your emphasis on accomplishments. Remember to appreciate people for what they are (patient, loving, fun to be with, kind) as well as what they do. The same technique can be used with parents, in-laws and other folks.

You can be creative with this exercise. One young woman had her father's positive characteristics inscribed on a photograph he loved. Other families have made this a game while they're traveling: "Okay, each one of us will tell what he/she likes about everyone in the car, one at a time."

SECRET # 3:

SHARE THE DIAMONDS

Years ago, Nick used an educational film in his marriage classes. Titled, "Johnny Lingo," it was a parable of a young man (Johnny Lingo) and a young woman (Mahanna) who lived far away on exotic, tropical islands.

Johnny was a handsome bachelor from a nearby island. Mahanna came from a good family and she had a pleasant personality, but she was shy and rather plain in appearance. However, Johnny saw her good qualities and fell in love with her. One day he arrived to ask to marry her.

In their custom, a prospective bridegroom brought a present of cows to the girl's father – as a measure of his devotion and the bride's desirability (worth) – usually three or four cows. An outstanding bride might fetch five or six cows. Mahanna's father expected to be offered two cows.

Johnny Lingo offered nine cows for the hand of Mahanna.

Johnny and Mahanna returned to his island after the wedding feast. Several months later, villagers saw Johnny arrive in his canoe. Who was the poised, beautiful woman with him? As she and Johnny walked through the village, people realized that the beauty was Mahanna – transformed from within by her new picture of herself.

The moral of this story is: Treat your spouse like a nine-cow person and see what happens.

A young woman from Germany shared:

Every Saturday my father goes to market, and he always brings home some beautiful flowers for my mother. It is really a sweet thing for him to do, and it makes my mother feel like a queen. The flowers have been a tradition since I was a child. Everyone in the family looks forward to them.

———

So often when we watch TV or a movie, my wife will say to me, "I'm glad you are the way you are. You're good to me and the kids; you don't drink; you're not so wrapped up in work that nothing else matters."

Then, too, as parents we teach our children their worth by what we tell them about themselves. They need to know that they are loveable, capable, and valuable. A fourteen-year-old told us:

> *My family moved from Oregon to Mississippi last year. We had to rent a truck, pack it, and do everything ourselves. I've never worked so hard or sweated so much. But my parents told me that they couldn't have done it without me. I overheard them telling other people, too. They really mean it.*

> *I like to read, and Mom and Dad are always happy when I finish another book. Sometimes they give me a treat, like going out for pizza.*

PUTTING IT TO WORK

Write birthday letters expressing your love.
Each year on the birthday of your spouse or children, give them a personal letter. Reminisce about things you did during the past year and tell them what you're especially proud of them for. Include a list of traits they possess that make you love them.

SECRET # 4:

ENCOURAGE THE EXPRESSION OF APPRECIATION AND AFFECTION

Life would be rosier if everyone – upon hearing of the importance of appreciation and affection – just started showing them. Doesn't work that way, though. Some folks grow up in families where little affection is shown; they aren't accustomed to hugs and pats on the shoulder. Others grow up knowing only criticism or "no comment."

To varying degrees, we all have to learn how to express appreciation and affection. And then sometimes we have to help a spouse or kids learn how.

> *During the first two years of our marriage, my husband was good about remembering our anniversary and my birthday. Then he sort of began to fade out. When he forgot our third anniversary, I was quite upset and cried all night. He brought me long-stemmed roses the next day, but I felt as if he'd only done it because I'd made a fuss.*
>
> *In the next several years, he forgot several anniversaries and birthdays, and we had a repeat of that third-anniversary scene. At a friend's suggestion, I decided to try a different approach.*
>
> *Here's what I do now: I begin pointing out the approach of events ahead of time. I do it casually and in good humor. I'll say something like, "That new Italian restaurant would be perfect to celebrate our anniversary next week."*

Children can learn from the example of their parents and by performing simple tasks of showing their gratitude to others. Gradually, they develop the habit of being appreciative for what others do for them – and then expressing it.

As one father said:

> *Many people don't bother to teach children even basic manners such as saying, "Thank you." They think children are too young. But that isn't so. My wife and I use good manners with each other and our children in everyday life. Our older son, when he was only about two, would say "dee doo" for "thank you."*

PUTTING IT TO WORK

Make giving compliments a daily goal.

Some people find it helpful to use a chart to remind themselves and to keep track of their progress. Although a bit mechanical, the chart can be an aid in getting the new behavior established. As expressing appreciation and affection becomes a habit, you won't need the chart.

Keep stationery and stamps to write thank-you notes.

Send them to friends and family for birthday and holiday gifts, a pleasant outing, dinner at their house, etc. They need not be long or eloquent. Children can do this as well.

SECRET # 5:

SHARE HUMOR AND PLAYFULNESS

I have been confined to our home for several years now due to an illness. I go out only rarely and then only in a wheelchair. Not long ago, I was having an especially bad time, very ill – and it was near my birthday. I've always been fond of bagpipe music; I guess that's just a little strange! My husband found someone in town who plays bagpipes and arranged for him to come over to our home. He stood outside my window and played a private little concert for me. Did I mention this was a surprise? I'll bet the neighbors never forget it either.

————

We found a long-forgotten box of family photos in the attic – with snapshots of my mother and dad taken in about 1943. Dad was in the army in the Pacific – quite handsome in his uniform and with such a lot of wavy hair. There were several of Mom that she had made to send to him – she's all dressed up in one. But the one that got everyone's attention is of her in a bathing suit and high heels in that classic Betty-Grable-pinup pose. For the fun of it, my husband had it enlarged (to 8x10) and framed.

Mom and Dad have had such a good time with these old photos. The grandkids (now in their twenties – same as Mom in the photo) asked, "Who's that?" when we showed the picture to them.

"Look close and you tell us."

After a pause, "GRANDMA?!"

The pictures of the "soldier boy" and his "pinup" have been shown to family, friends, and neighbors. Folks of their age relive and share their own war memories; younger folks are given a bit of history and romance. Theirs is a sweet story – married just before he left for overseas for over two years and still married sixty years later. Mom explains, "I wanted him to have his own pinup – to remind him of who was waiting at home." When people tell them that they were a handsome couple, Dad tells them (with a laugh), "Well, we haven't always looked the way we do today. It takes time to achieve this!"

Strong families tend to use a lot of positive humor. They enjoy each other's company, they like to laugh and tell stories, they like to play together, and they express affection with gentle humor. But two kinds of "humor" – sarcasm and put-downs – are not related to strength in families. In fact, sarcasm and put-downs are not really humor at all. They are verbal weapons used to dominate people, show power, and establish control.

PUTTING IT TO WORK

Collect funny family stories.

Most families have those stories that live through the years and make everyone laugh. Stories like the camping trip when the sudden thunderstorm's winds ripped a hole in the tent. And how, as we fled to the car, brother stepped on the milk jug, squashing it and spraying milk everywhere. And then we wonder where that tent finally ended up – Is it still in Montana somewhere or is it east of the Mississippi yet?

Forgo negative "humor".

Ask, "Is this funny to everyone involved?" Be watchful of areas that may be sensitive or embarrassing such as weight or age. You may find Uncle's falling out of the fishing boat funny, but he may feel foolish.

SECRET # 6:
ACCEPT EXPRESSIONS OF APPRECIATION GRACEFULLY

We've all had it happen to us. Someone does something you like or looks especially nice and you say, "Your speech was excellent" or "That dress is beautiful." And the recipient of your praise replies, "Really? I thought it was too long" or "This old thing? I never liked the color."

And there you stand, feeling stupid.

> *My wife grew up in a family where compliments were scarce. Whenever I'd praise her – on her cooking, for example – she'd say, "I know you like it, because you ate it."*

> *Our twins have hit that awkward pre-teen stage: they don't know how they want to behave. They eat it up when someone admires their clothes or tells them they've done a good job in ballet. And yet they're embarrassed. They don't want to appear to be puffed up, so sometimes they are silly and giggle or say the wrong thing.*

Many of us are uncomfortable as the recipients of praise or compliments. We don't wish to appear immodest or don't care for the spotlight. However, not accepting expressions of gratitude or appreciation correctly can be interpreted as a rebuff and may stymie future overtures of appreciation. Members of strong families realize that the ability to receive appreciation gracefully is critical to keeping it flowing.

PUTTING IT TO WORK

Practice to be a gracious recipient of compliments.

Some people plan some phrases that they can use when someone praises them. They may say, "Thank you for telling me" or "How kind of you to notice" or "What a nice thing to say." Or they may respond with a simple, "Thanks" and a genuine smile. You won't appear haughty; you will make the person complimenting you feel good. This preparation is especially helpful for those times when you can't think of anything to say.

CHAPTER SIX
TIME TOGETHER

The ice storm made travel perilous and virtually impossible. Normal activities halted for three days: Schools and businesses shut down. Some were frustrated by the inconvenience and interruption of daily routines. Not eight-year-old Elizabeth! She was delighted.

She had both of her parents at home They couldn't go to work or to run errands, So they kept a warm fire going in the fireplace; they read stories and played games; they explored the ice-coated world outside. They had popcorn and hot chocolate – "as much as we wanted." As the ice thawed and life began to get back to normal, Elizabeth said to her parents, "These have been the best days of my life."

What an important message from the heart of a child!

In surveys where children are asked, "What do you think makes a happy family?" they also astonish us with their wisdom. Their most common answer is NOT money, cars, television, or even video games. The answer they give most frequently is doing things together – the very reason that Elizabeth proclaimed the three days of the ice storm the best days of her life.

A family that spends time together reaps valuable benefits. First, communication is improved.

My wife understands all our two-year-old's jabber because the two of them spend lots of time together. Margaret was there when little Lyn named rabbits "raboos." Lyn calls alligators "cup" because she has a drinking cup with an alligator on it. It makes sense when you know the details. It's like that in other areas of communication. You have to spend time with people to know them and to talk with them *to get beyond the superficial matters. Some families I know aren't face-to-face long enough each week to discuss football scores and the weather much less get on to matters of heart and mind.*

Spending time together as a family is a powerful antidote to isolation, loneliness, and alienation. Members of strong families know they are liked and wanted; they know they'll never be abandoned.

We enjoy each other's company. Frankly, I get lonesome for my husband and kids when we're apart for very long.

———

I had a disturbing experience when I was forty-three years old. I lost a battle with a hepatitis bug and was confined at home for several months to recuperate. My colleagues at work called to inquire about me at first and then drifted away. Except for two close friends and my family, everyone else forgot about my difficulties in a hurry. I don't blame them, and I'm not bitter or complaining. I've been guilty of the same thing myself. What the experience did was make me realize which people are truly important to me. I'm really fortunate to have a wife, daughters, mother (my dad is dead), a brother, in-laws, and a few close friends who care. Spending time with these folks isn't a luxury; it's a necessity. They save me from being lost and alone.

A third benefit of spending time together is that the family develops its own identity – a group unity and a sense of their place in history.

Photographs are very important to us. We have albums and albums, plus a huge box of them that need to be put in albums. All the important events in our family have been recorded – our wedding, the births and growth of the children, vacations, first days of school, new cars and houses, pets, and on it goes. The kids love to look at the pictures and see what they looked like as babies; our seventeen-year-old looks remarkably like her mother's wedding photo – when she was twenty.

In this part of the country, tornadoes occasionally wipe houses completely out. I've thought that if that ever happened to us, the material thing I would miss most would be our family photographs.

Members of strong families offer some suggestions for spending time together.

SUGGESTION # 1:
MAKE TIME TO MAKE MEMORIES

Take a short journey back to your childhood. Relax in a comfy chair, kick off your shoes, and close your eyes. Think back. Way back to when you were a child. What are some of the happiest memories of your family life in your childhood? Spend a few moments in your travel back in time before you resume.

Through interviews and questionnaires, many strong families took the same journey you just did. Following are some very common examples of what they remembered:

I remember stories Mom and Dad told me when they tucked me in bed.

———

Going with Dad to work on the farm. I felt so important – so superior, because my little brother wasn't big enough to go. Every few weeks, Dad and I would scoop out the pig barn, and we'd talk and talk. It was great.

———

Having the whole family together at Christmas was special. All the grandpas and grandmas and aunts and uncles and thousands of kids. They made us kids eat in the kitchen together. I thought it was so neat then, but it must have been pandemonium.

———

Singing together. Yes, singing. We had an old piano, and I learned to play, and we would all sing corny songs.

———

Vacation. We would go fifty miles to the lake and rent a cabin. A cheap cabin. And Dad would swim with us and dunk me.

———

My dad and I would cook Sunday lunch together. We were all too busy during the week to take much time, but Sundays, Dad and I would make something special like hamburgers or bean sandwiches.

Now that you've read other people's stories about their best childhood memories and considered your own, you'll notice at least two important things. First, years and years later, the times we adults remember about our childhood – those happiest memories – are times spent with our loved ones simply doing things together.

Second, you'll find that our best memories rarely have anything to do with money. In American society, we are bombarded by messages urging us to spend and to consume. And yet, when thousands of people told us about their happiest childhood memories, hardly anyone told a story about something that cost the family a lot of money. Sometimes they were on vacation, but usually they were camping or staying at a budget motel. Only rarely did someone tell about visiting an expensive theme park or vacation "paradise." And only ONCE did someone describe a super memory of their family eating a fancy meal together in an expensive restaurant.

Now, think what memories you are creating for your children by the lifestyle you currently live. What will they remember years from now?

PUTTING IT TO WORK

Write down, tape record, or video tape your family's history.

Involve grandparents and older relatives. Ask grandparents questions such as "What were your parents' and grandparents' names?" "Where did they live?" "Where are they buried?" "Where did you live as a child?" "What occupations did these folks follow?" "Who are your brothers and sisters?" "How did you and your spouse meet, court, marry?" "What are the names of your children?" "When and where were they born?" "Where did you attend school?" "How did you celebrate holidays, birthdays, harvests, weddings, as a child?"

For the immediate family include information about places of residence, circumstances surrounding the birth of each child, vacations, special events, and hobbies. Use pictures if possible. A family reunion can be a good place to find out interesting bits of family history.

SUGGESTION # 2:
Do Everyday Things Together

Members of strong families use meal times and the time needed to run a household as opportunities to share time together.

> *We eat the evening meal together. In extreme cases, one of us may not be there, but everyone knows that being absent from dinner is not taken lightly. We use that time to share triumphs and tribulations. In a hectic world, we need some common ground where we can meet.*

> ———

> *I work until late in the afternoon, so I need help getting dinner ready. At first my son protested about having to cook, but I've convinced him that there may be many times when knowing how to cook will be handy.*
> *Now he's proud of his accomplishments. He often has cookies or a cake ready before I get home.*
> *Our daughter is still a little young to handle very hot things or knives but she sets the table and likes to make simple vegetable or fruit salads.*
> *We all get in the kitchen and talk about what went on at school and work while we fix dinner. They're learning other valuable things besides cooking; they're learning they are important in making our family run.*

> ———

> *Nearly every Saturday morning we have a clean-up session at the house. We all pitch in to help: Somebody vacuums; somebody dusts; somebody empties trash. We run a couple loads of laundry. It's a real swirl of activity for a couple hours. Then we're done and ready to have some fun. Plus the house is tidied up.*

PUTTING IT TO WORK

Remember quality and quantity.

Family members need lots of time together. George Rekers, family therapist, points out that if you order an expensive steak at a restaurant and your waiter serves a two-inch cube of meat ("Our best quality!"), you will know that quantity also counts.

Actually, quality and quantity go hand in hand. Time together needs to be good – no one enjoys hours of bickering, arguing, pouting, or bullying. But time also needs to be of sufficient quantity – quality interaction just isn't likely to develop in a few minutes here and there.

SUGGESTION # 3:

ENJOY RELIGIOUS, CLUB, AND SCHOOL ACTIVITIES TOGETHER

Our son's kindergarten teacher has a plan to use parent volunteers in the classroom. One time I supervised the art center; another time I read to small groups of the kids. We also helped with the rehearsal for their winter holiday program.

———

The Band Boosters have a concession stand at the football games (as a fund raiser). I've gotten good at grilling burgers and making nachos. It's fun when the kids stop by.

Strong families report that activities at school, scouting, sports leagues, and 4-H often involve the entire family. If the children have a band concert, recital, or are in a program, mom and dad and the family are in the audience.

Families often attend worship services together. They are involved in activities such as discussion groups, family game night, or service projects such as food distribution to poor families

SUGGESTION # 4:
SPEND SPECIAL EVENTS TOGETHER

These include holidays, vacations, and personal observances such as birthdays. Members of strong families regard these as times when the entire family should be together.

Birthdays are big events at our home. We have a special meal and cake. The birthday person gets presents, of course. We also have added our own twist. The birthday person gives small presents to family members as a way of thanking them for enriching his or her life.

——

Holidays are special times. We enjoy decorating the house, fixing special foods. We have traditions for most holidays such as jack-o-lanterns at Halloween, a food basket for a needy family at Thanksgiving, sunrise service at Easter, a trip to the cemetery on Memorial Day.

——

Our vacations are planned with everyone in the family in mind. We try to work in antique or craft shops for Mom, some fishing for Dad, and amusement parks or swimming for the children.

PUTTING IT TO WORK

Designate one wall or room for family mementos.
Hang pictures of Mom and Dad, the kids, the pets, grandparents, houses you lived in before, favorite vacation spots, etc. Decorate the room with souvenirs of trips – shells from the beach, for example. The room may not win any awards for interior design, but the furnishings will have meaning for your family. A feeling of family identity will be created. Many happy memories will be stirred.

Work together to design a family symbol or logo.
Have it printed on T-shirts or jackets so that everyone in the family has matching jackets or shirts. Put the design on a flag for the house or a banner for the front door.

SUGGESTION # 5:
DO NOTHING IN PARTICULAR

When I was growing up, there was a mimosa tree in our yard. It was large and umbrella-like, with fragrant pink flowers in the summer. We – Mom, Sis, and I – would spread a blanket under the tree, stretch out and watch the hummingbirds that came for the nectar from its blossoms. You had to lie very still, and of course, you couldn't talk or the hummers wouldn't come. We spent many warm, drowsy afternoons there, doing nothing in particular.

Recognize the value and benefit of being with members of your family and not doing anything in particular. Sit on the deck in the late evening and watch fireflies; listen to the rain. Put some miles on a porch swing or rocking chairs. Meander along the creek or pond; wade a little; skip some stones. Stretch out in the grass and watch the clouds drift by or watch for shooting stars at night.

We don't have to do anything in particular in order to enjoy each other's company. We can be content doing nothing except savoring family closeness.

PUTTING IT TO WORK

Serendipity is a fun word.

It means finding good things that were not sought. Much of the good that comes from time spent together is serendipitous. It springs naturally from the moment. It has been said that we as humans should live each day "as if it were a prayer." Each moment of our lives together is a verse of this daily prayer. By living life from sacred moment to sacred moment, we are aware of the potential joy waiting to be found in each of these fleeting moments. Instead of being lost in the race to accomplish, we can enjoy the sunshine of our pleasant saunter through life.

It was early spring at the beach and unexpectedly, bitter cold. We decided to bundle up and take one short walk before going home. We drove a few miles to a section of Gulf Islands National Seashore, pulled into the empty parking lot, and were immediately greeted by a flock of seagulls. As we got out, we tossed some snack leftovers. In a flash, we were in a cloud of seagulls. Caught up in the fun of it, we fed the gulls a box of saltines, a loaf of bread, and a box of Moon-pie cakes from our picnic supplies. They'd hover just above our heads and catch the goodies we tossed. I've never seen gulls so close; sometimes their wings brushed our hair.

SUGGESTION # 6:
PLAY TOGETHER

A large number of the strong families mentioned outdoor activities as favorite ways to be together. Many play catch or yard games. They camp, canoe, hike, picnic, stargaze, play league sports, bicycle, walk, and swim. Their responses give clues to the allure of the outdoors.

We love to canoe a little river not far from here. The appeal to me is the beauty of the spot. After a day of sunlight on the leaves, fresh air, the ripple of the water, my soul is refreshed. My husband says he feels more in touch with the eternally important things. He gains perspective. Petty trials come and go, but the river flows on. The kids have a blast swimming, collecting rocks, hunting fossils, and stalking frogs.

———

We have a special town on the Gulf Coast that is a favorite of ours. We camp and fish and go crabbing. There are no phones or televisions. For a couple of days, the outside world disappears. What a pleasure it is to get up when we want, eat when we're hungry, and be free of schedules.

Many strong families also mentioned indoor recreation.

Every Friday night we rent some movies and make nachos.

———

We enjoy board games such as Monopoly or Scrabble, telling stories, or reading aloud as a change from television.

———

We do jigsaw puzzles as a family fun pursuit. The only problem is that it's hard to leave a good puzzle. Once or twice we've lost track of the time until 2:00 A.M., so we try to be really careful on school nights.

PUTTING IT TO WORK

Control television, computer, video games.

TV, video games, and computers can interrupt family life, demanding too much attention and bringing influences that are not good (violence, sex, etc.). You may wish to set strict limits on how much time is spent in these pursuits and on the nature of programs watched.

Filters are available to screen certain sites from computer access. Keep TV, video games, and the computer in a location where mom and dad can monitor – in the den rather than in children's bedrooms, for example.

Another approach is to improve the time spent watching TV. Turn down the volume during commercials and discuss what you've seen. Or discuss the commercials, "Will this shampoo really make you more popular?" "In beer commercials everyone is happy, young, and attractive. How realistic is that?"

CHAPTER SEVEN
MUSIC

Music is melody for the soul. Music soothes emotional wounds. Music encourages and lifts up our spirits. It can bring rhythm and joy to our lives.

There is another fact about music that you may not know. Like a treasure buried deep in the forest, it is there for the taking, but few are aware of its existence. Music can help build more harmonious family relationships!

Why do we single out music from the many other wonderful activities that strong families participate in together — such as sports, camping, art, board games, or photography? Because music is unique in the way in which it brings families together. Because music is holistic in nature, involving the mind, reasoning, emotions, and the body. And because of the enthusiasm and frequency with which families reported music as a source of joy and togetherness.

Although sharing music is not a separate, seventh quality of strong families, a number of families in our national and international research share that music plays an important role in contributing to their family strengths. Based on what strong families tell us and based upon what many other researchers have found, there are some important benefits of music to your family.

BENEFIT # 1:

BRAIN DEVELOPMENT

A newborn baby's brain is composed of trillions of neurons (brain cells). The experiences of childhood determine which neurons are used (firing electrical impulses to other neurons) and thus wiring the circuits of the brain.   Neurons that are not used may die.

A baby's brain is constantly building new connections by the stimuli that the baby receives – the sight of a toy or mom's face, the smell of cinnamon rolls baking, the sounds of a tune that dad sings. The more connections formed, the more successful the brain is in handling any new information it receives.*

When a young child first experiences music, a new pathway is constructed that will be available the next time a similar musical experience arises. Recent research is showing that people are "pre-wired" to receive and decipher musical stimuli. For example, unborn babies can hear songs in the womb and will stop sucking in order to listen more closely when the same familiar songs are played for them.

One of the earliest and most critical stages of a child's musical development occurs during the first six years. This is the time when the brain is learning to make sense of and order the sounds of music. Many studies show that the musical ability of children raised in a home rich in musical experiences far surpasses the musical ability of children reared in a home lacking this richness.*

Musical experiences in early childhood not only contribute to the child's musical abilities but also contribute greatly to the child's intellectual development in other ways:

- Gordon Shaw and other researchers propose that music may be considered a "pre-language" and that early music experiences may be useful in exercising the brain for higher cognitive functions.

- At-risk children who participated in an arts program that included music showed significant increases in self-concept.

- Preschool children given music training demonstrate significant improvement in spatial reasoning ability.

- Preschoolers showed a 46% increase in their spatial reasoning and IQ following eight months of keyboard lessons.

- Students in two Rhode Island elementary schools who were given a sequential, skill-building music program demonstrated a marked improvement in math skills.

- Preschool children who studied piano performed 34% better in spatial and temporal reasoning ability than did children who spent the same amount of time learning to use computers.**

Musical experiences in the preschool years provide an extremely important foundation for a child's music education. The listening vocabulary of music should begin to be formed before a child is eighteen months old and not later than three years of age.**

*Chinn, J. (2003). *Music and Young Children: Preparing the Brain for a Lifetime of Learning*. Growing Up In Santa Cruz.
http://growing-up.com/music.html

**Pratt, D. (2003). *Music Is Important for Young Children*.
The Music Education Madness Site.
http://www.musiceducationmadness.com/important.shtml

PUTTING IT TO WORK

Sing to your baby even before she is born.

Make music for your unborn baby. Remember he is listening!

Continue singing and making music after baby is born.

Even if you don't think you're a great (or good) singer, sing to baby and remember to make eye contact. Often maintain a warm physical touch such as cuddling or holding hands. Choose soothing music such as lullabies or waltzes. Use a variety of music; it doesn't have to be all children's songs. Try to offer music that your baby may eventually be able to coo back to you; young babies are able to imitate sounds and love the game of back and forth imitation with mom or dad.

When your baby becomes a toddler, encourage her to sing along and do the movements to songs such as "Row, Row, Row Your Boat," "Twinkle, Twinkle Little Star," "The Wheels on the Bus," and "Old MacDonald." At this age children love to make the movements and the simple steps to their favorite songs. They love to "dance" to all kinds of music. They enjoy it even more when you participate with them.

It is important to remember that you need not feel that you must teach your preschooler the "correct" way to do these activities. Nor do you need to worry if your singing voice leaves something to be desired and you wobble when you "dance." Simply allow yourself and your child to enjoy music. Have fun! Your child's musical abilities are being developed and in the process, the bond between you and your child is being strengthened.

You can provide your child with early childhood music programs such as Suzuki, Kindermusik, and Music Together. These three specific programs all emphasize the importance of parental involvement.

BENEFIT # 2:
SHARED FAMILY TIME

"Some of my happiest childhood memories of my family involve music," shares Tula, a grandmother who has been part of three generations of strong families.

"There was always music in our home. My father played the violin (Technically, I guess you'd say he played the fiddle.) and guitar. He taught me to play the guitar; I tried the fiddle, but didn't do as well with it. Having my dad teach me to play brought us closer to each other. Even when he was an old man and ill, we'd reminisce about those times – how good they had been.

"But, I want you to understand that we didn't have scheduled lesson times or anything like that. Mostly this was very informal. And we all looked forward to it. Usually what happened was that my dad would pick up his fiddle and I'd grab the guitar. He and I might play a few tunes together – he'd offer some suggestions – teach me some new skills. We'd play our 'old favorites' and also work on some new songs, too.

"In the evenings and on weekends other family members would hear us. They'd come and join in with singing along. They might drift in one at a time, but everybody got there eventually and then we'd really sing up a storm. We had quite a repertoire of songs that we knew – parts and all. Mom had a fine alto voice. My younger brother and sister would make up their own dance moves and dance to the music.

"It was such fun! And I think the music brought us together in a way that nothing else did. When we made music together, we were relaxed. No problems to wrestle with. No time schedule. We could simply enjoy being together."

The most commonly mentioned benefit of music to the family which was reported by the strong families (who specifically mentioned music or music-related activities) was that it is shared family time. It is something enjoyable that the family does together. As a result it can strengthen the bonds between family members.

For many families, music becomes the focus for traditions which may be celebrated on a daily or weekly basis. These traditions sometimes evolve into a couple or family adopting a song that becomes "their song."

> *Ned and I enjoy listening to the Platters. Oops! I guess I really dated myself with that, didn't I? No matter! Our favorite Platters song is "Only You" – which we sing to each other on our anniversaries and birthdays or other special occasions.*
>
> *We enjoy singing the words of this song to each other because of the special meaning to us. We also laugh a lot because neither of us is a very good singer. So this is a nice mixture of very sweet and just a little silly.*
>
> > *Only you can make the darkness light.*
> > *Only you can make the world seem right.*
> > *Only you and you alone*
> > *Can thrill me like you do;*
> > *And fill my life with dreams of only you.*

> *Being a Kentucky family, our enjoyment of Bluegrass music goes back several generations. We listen to it and also play. The banjo is my instrument.*
>
> *There is one song that we have had so much fun with that it has become our family song. The song is titled, "How Many Biscuits Did You Eat This Morning?" It has a peppy rhythm and funny lyrics – and since we all like biscuits, it just naturally became "our" song.*

PUTTING IT TO WORK

Incorporate music into your family time.

Sing when you travel together. If someone in the family plays a musical instrument, sings, or dances, include performing into family night. Sing together or play together at extended family gatherings. Attend concerts or recitals as a family. Listen to music together – at home, in the car. Consider finding a song to be your family's "theme song."

BENEFIT # 3:

AN EFFECTIVE STRESS RELIEVER

Many families report that music benefits them as a family by helping to reduce stress. Music is greatly underrated as a stress fighter.

> *We live in Iowa and our parents live in northern Florida. Because we want our kids to have as much contact with their grandparents as possible, we travel back and forth at least a couple times each year. It is a long drive, but I don't mind most of it. We do have to go through several large cities and I don't like those – they're stressful to me. And, for some reason, St. Louis is the worst – the traffic always seems heavy and something is always under construction. I'm usually tense and irritable by the time we get halfway through town.*
>
> *On one trip, I had brought a new CD of some Straus waltzes – they're a favorite of mine. The kids were busy in the back seat and my wife was napping so I put in the CD just as we were coming into St. Louis. I guess I soon fell under the mood of the music, because traffic seemed to move smoothly. I could glide in and out as I needed to keep moving. I didn't feel tense or frustrated.*
>
> *About halfway through, my wife woke up, surprised that we were that far along and that I wasn't fuming and fussing. I told her that this was the easiest that St. Louis had ever been. She agreed that it seemed as if I were driving with a certain rhythm and smoothness – as if we truly had "waltzed" through St. Louis. Yes, pun intended. But I keep my trusty Straus waltz CD handy when we travel!*

Playing a musical instrument is an effective way of reducing stress for many individuals. For example, one mother has found this to be true for her teenager:

> *My daughter is fifteen and has all the hormone changes and other trials that teens go through. When she feels anxious or depressed, she will often play the piano. She may spend a few minutes or a few hours; sometimes she plays her own melodies. I guess she*

feels this is a way of expressing her feelings. And it helps her to heal because she always is calmer and more optimistic when she finishes.

She began taking lessons when she was only six years old. I never dreamed then that one of the benefits would be that the music would help her to manage stress.

Kareem, a young father in Detroit, talked about teaching his son and daughter to "sing a happy song" whenever they felt worried or frustrated:

I knew this habit would work for them because it has worked for me. I learned it from my grandmother, a woman of great spiritual faith. When I would get discouraged or anxious, I would go to her for help. She and I would sit down and talk about the best way to approach the problem. She was so wise and I could tell her anything that was on my mind.

After we figured out the best way to handle my problem, she'd remind me to "sing a joyful song." She'd say, "Kareem, God wants you to be happy. You can be, too. It's just hard not to feel good when you sing a happy song." One of her favorite scriptures was from the 98th Psalm, the first and fourth verses:

"O Sing unto the Lord a new song for he hath done marvelous things…"

"Make a joyful noise unto the Lord, all the earth: Make a loud noise, and rejoice and sing praise."

She often reminded me that many people make themselves more frustrated and miserable because they were "singing the wrong song." She meant they had a negative attitude. But I took her advice to heart and made a habit of singing a joyful song. Sometimes for me it is a gospel song – either an old hymn or something contemporary – or it might be a popular, secular song. Either way it helps me to keep a better, more up-beat attitude.

It is really no surprise that singing, playing a musical instrument, or listening to music can be an effective stress reducer. Music involves the mind, imagery, reasoning, emotions, and the body.

Because of its holistic nature, music is used as an intervention for various kinds of difficulties and as an aid in personal growth. Music therapy is successfully used in such areas as improving communication and relationship skills, improving fine motor skills, pain management, stress management, autism, Alzheimer's, and behavioral problems.

Bill Anderson, who has professional expertise in music education and educational psychology, shares an interesting experience that happened while he was working with a group of patients with Alzheimer's.

Bill and a team of other professionals were using music therapy as part of the overall program. Every day the team would gather with the patients and play music. Bill would play his guitar and lead the group in singing songs which may have been favorites of these older patients when they were teenagers. For some reason, we tend to remember really well the songs and music of our adolescence.

One older man who was in the advanced stages of Alzheimer's never responded to any of the songs. He always sat with his head bowed down. No one was surprised; he hadn't spoken in over four years.

Then one eventful afternoon, Bill led the group in singing "Take Me Out to the Ball Game." Suddenly the man who had been silent for so long began to SING. Everyone else was so shocked that they all stopped singing. The older man continued to sing all by himself – every line of the song!

The melody and words of "Take Me Out to the Ball Game" represented something he had learned and cherished as a young man. This song connected with him in a way that nothing else had.

PUTTING IT TO WORK

Use music to reduce tension.

Find a CD or tape of music that you find relaxing – perhaps something soft and mellow. Listen to it at the end of the day to help you to relax and let the day's tensions unravel. If you play a musical instrument, spend a few minutes each day playing; see if your stress level goes down.

BENEFIT # 4:
A SPIRITUAL CONNECTION

Music is a language that goes beyond letters, words, and verbal communication, according to Shinichi Suzuki, founder of the world-famous Talent Education Research Institute. He further stated that music is a living art that is almost mystical.

Music can inspire and lift us up. At times, music connects with the inner being – the spirit. Perhaps this is one reason why music therapy is often successful – it has a spiritual dimension.

At age thirty, Allen, the father of two daughters, began a five-year period of what he termed a "living hell" of severe depression. He elaborated:

> *Many times during that trip through hell, I was so sick I could not function. I mean I couldn't get out of bed some days. I didn't want to see anyone or do anything. I'd stare at the ceiling or sleep.*
>
> *My wife and daughters were responsible for getting me through the depression. Their love and support was critical; they didn't ever give up on me. That means more to me than I could ever express.*
>
> *There was something else that was a major reason why I overcame the depression – music therapy. I began by listening to spiritual music – mostly hymns. At first I didn't have the energy to do anything other than listen. But I soaked it up. I would feel better afterwards – at first only for a few minutes, but then longer and longer.*
>
> *One day I felt a stirring to play music again. I had been a professional organist before the depression incapacitated me. So I began to play again.*
>
> *I don't think I can explain what happened other than to say that it was a spiritual experience for me. Somehow playing the music healed my broken spirit. An important part of that healing came as I began to do some creative things with the hymns. I'd take a phrase or a part of the melody from a favorite hymn and weave it in with some music of my own composing (that I felt expressed my feelings about the hymn).*

Some of the songs turned out very nicely. Others who heard them encouraged me to record them. We have just finished an album that I hope will help other people.

The idea that music has a spiritual connection is also illustrated in *Nurtured by Love* by an encounter which the great violin teacher, Shinichi Suzuki, had with the mother of one of his students. The student was doing well in his lessons, but the mother inquired, "Sensei {Teacher}, will my boy amount to something?"

Suzuki laughed and answered, "No. He will not become something." Suzuki felt that her question reflected a cold, calculating educational attitude which many parents possess.

Suzuki observed that the mother was surprised by his answer so he continued, "He will become a noble person through his violin playing. Isn't that enough? You should stop wanting your child to become a professional, just a good money earner. This thought is concealed in your question and is offensive. A person with a fine and pure heart will find happiness. The only worry for parents should be to bring up their children as noble human beings. That is sufficient. If this is not their greatest hope, in the end the child may take a road contrary to their expectations. Your son plays the violin very well. We must try to make him splendid in mind and heart also."

BENEFIT # 5:

STRENGTHENS THE PARENT-CHILD BOND

Experiencing music together can strengthen the parent-child bond and do it in a pleasant way. This is the testimony of many families. It is not surprising that many families report this to be true. Harmony, rhythm, joy, peacefulness, and relaxation – as well as many other qualities are experienced together through music. When good things are shared, parent and child grow closer to each other.

Another dimension is added to the parent-child relationship when the parent is involved in the child's learning to play a musical instrument. Two mothers share their stories:

> *I spend a lot of time being involved in my son's music lessons. I go with him to his lessons with his teacher and I make sure he practices at home. That takes a lot of time, but I try to encourage him by listening and commenting on his improvement. Or I might ask him to play a song that he learned earlier on. I don't hover over him, but I want him to know that I'm interested. Of course I attend all of his recitals and concerts.*
>
> *I believe this has enriched my relationship with my son. We're learning together and having some fun too. I'm very proud of him and he knows it.*
>
> ———
>
> *We chose a teacher who uses the Suzuki method for teaching violin for our daughter's lessons. I was a bit surprised to learn that I had to "go first." I knew I would attend all her lessons, but didn't realize that this teacher started out by having me learn the basics of the violin first. My daughter watched me play before she was allowed to imitate me and play the violin.*

Many music educators believe that it is critical for children to see their parents being musical so that they will be encouraged to play music. Perhaps even more important is the principle that when parents are involved in musical activities and experiences with their children, it can strengthen the parent-child bond.

BENEFIT # 6:

JUST PLAIN FUN

It was our first trip to Austria and we were enjoying the beautiful, historic city of Vienna. Friends who lived there took us out to dinner one evening. As we strolled through a commercial district on the way to our dinner destination, we passed a café. Sounds of melodious, happy singing emanated from within and caught my attention.

I commented to our friends that they had a good band playing at the café. Our friends were amused and told us that it was no band. What we heard was just a family and friends who were having dinner and singing together. It is common in Austria for families to sing together – even when they're out in a restaurant – as part of a pleasant evening. We were impressed at the joy and openness with which families joined in this custom.

A greatly underestimated value of music to the family is simply the fun and joy it can bring. Living in our families should be joyful. The common belief that happiness is a result of circumstances can prevent us from realizing that there is much that we can do to make joy happen.

We can create the climate in which joyful experiences can become a part of daily family life. One way that many strong families do this is by making music together. They report that one of the benefits of music to their family is not the perfection of playing but just the fun of playing together.

I play the clarinet and my sister plays the flute. We are both in the high school band. A while back we found a book of clarinet – flute duets. We have had so much fun playing duets. We may do this an entire afternoon or evening. We keep at it until the piece sounds the way we want.

And then sometimes just for the heck of it, we will switch instruments. Of course, I'm not as good with the flute and she isn't as good with the clarinet. So she pinches the reed and squeaks and we both forget the fingerings. At these times, our dog, Pinkie, usual-ly shows up and starts howling. It can get pretty funny; we end up laughing more than playing.

PART THREE
CREATING A STRONG FAMILY

A strong family is made up of people who love and
care for each other always and regardless.

In Parts One and Two you have learned about the six characteristics of strong families. Commitment, spiritual well-being, and the ability to cope with stress and crises all work together to help families to endure. Positive communication and conflict resolution, generous amounts of appreciation and affection, and high-quality time together make strong families pleasant, happy places to live.

The next step in creating a stronger family can be taken by assessing your family's strengths. Then your family can envision a better family life and can create a practical action plan to achieve your goals.

CHAPTER EIGHT
MAKING YOUR FAMILY STRONGER

You can make your family stronger, happier, and healthier by applying the six principles shared in this book. If you already live in a strong, happy family – you can safeguard that treasure and make it even stronger. But what if your family isn't faring so well? What if it is besieged with communication problems, infidelity, lack of interest, alcohol or drug abuse, or family violence?

Can struggling families become strong and healthy? Well, can people change? The answer to both questions, of course, is YES! People change every day. And families can too.

Too often we operate under the assumption that people who are successful have always been that way. Not so. Did you know that Margaret Mitchell received numerous rejections of her manuscript for *Gone With The Wind*? Some were quite nasty and even advised her to do a complete rewrite. Or were you aware that Albert Einstein did not pass his college entrance exams?

Just as famous and successful people were not always famous or successful, so families that are now strong may not always have been that way. Many happy, strong families were once mediocre or troubled. More than a few have been on the verge of breaking up.

Countless families have overcome communication problems, infidelity, lack of interest, alcohol or drug abuse, family violence or a host of other difficulties to become healthy, strong families. If they can do it, your family can too.

As you know or might guess, strong families are not built overnight or with leftover energy. It takes work, effort, and time. However, as the families in our research have said time and time again – the effort is well worth it.

If you are ready to become all you can be as a family, the following action steps will help put what you've learned into practice.

ACTION STEP # 1:
Assess Your Family's Strengths

Many families are unaware of their strengths and, instead, focus on their weaknesses and difficulties. When you are aware of your family's strengths and resources, you can more effectively deal with the problems that come along. And you can enjoy your family along the way.

Use the tool, "Assessing Your Family's Strengths" in Appendix A of this book to gain greater insight into your family. When each family member completes the assessment, share your answers with one another. You will get a good idea of where your family's strengths are. You will also gain an awareness of areas requiring some improvement.

Use this tool with honesty, but with gentleness and understanding. Remember that no family is perfect. In your family discussion, don't argue or try to convince another family member to change his or her assessment. The most important thing is to use this tool to identify the strengths already in existence in your family and the areas in which you wish to develop greater strength. Rather than concentrating on the characteristics that are weak or lacking, rejoice in the resources you already have.

ACTION STEP # 2:
CREATE A FAMILY VISION

After you use the assessment to get a snapshot of what your family looks like now, the next step is to get a vision of what you want the family to become. Involve all family members who are old enough in this process. Ask them to write the answers to some questions. Then you will compare and discuss your answers.

Ask first, "What do you want our family to do?" Perhaps it is to play together more, or to spend more time together, or to laugh more. Some families have some specific visions such as to have a house with enough land for horses.

Next ask, "What do you want our family to be?" Perhaps it is to be happy, peaceful, or supportive of each other. Maybe it is to be a family that is helpful to others. Whatever it is, write your desires on a piece of paper.

Now share your visualizations with each other. Combine them to create a family vision statement that incorporates most of the desired goals expressed by family members.

The process of creating your family vision statement can be very rewarding to your family. It puts into words the very important goals and desires for your life together.

You may wish to have the final product written nicely – and perhaps decorated – and framed. Hang it prominently in your home as a reminder of what you want your family to become. It will become a guide to your family. You may well find that your family becomes much like the vision statement.

ACTION STEP # 3:
MAKE A FAMILY STRENGTHS ACTION PLAN

Now – based on your family vision – it is time to make some specific goals and the strategies for achieving them (to get down to the nitty gritty!). For example, if one of your goals is to have more fun together, have a brainstorming session. Ask family members, "What are things we enjoy doing for fun?" "What are activities that you think we might enjoy?" Some of the activities might happen on a daily basis while others might be weekly. Some may happen less often, such as a family rafting trip or vacation in the mountains.

You can appoint a "family action plan" captain who will coordinate your planning. He or she can set times and dates for activities, with each family member's cooperation, of course. Family members will need to commit to participate in the activities. Revise the plan as needed.

It may be helpful for you to use an action plan revolving around the six characteristics of strong families. Use the Family Strengths Action Plan in Appendix B of this book to help you to achieve your goals. Try it!

ACTION STEP # 4:
COMMIT

Building a strong, happy family is a process – not a one-time event. Implementing what you know to do to improve your family takes a long-term commitment. It means changing the way you think about your family and the way you behave. It may mean starting over after mistakes or discouragement. It means changing priorities.

But this isn't a grim, unpleasant process. One of the great things about the six characteristics of strong families is that they all interact with each other in dynamic and powerful ways. As you put your family plan into action, you won't see a change in only one area at a time. You'll find that as you improve in one area, other areas will improve as well. It is a holistic process – a circle of power for your family.

For example, as family members grow in commitment to the family, they will spend more time with one another. Commitment also enables the family to pull together in a crisis and to work at improving communication.

Family members who spend pleasant time together reinforce commitment and communication.

Expressed appreciation and affection reinforce commitment.

Good communication is necessary in crises and in resolving conflict and in expressing appreciation.

Spiritual well-being is critical to coping with stress and crises, to appreciating the value of people, to valuing time together, and to being committed to each other.

It's all part of the ongoing process.

THE BEGINNING

A man and his young son walked along the beach. They stopped to gaze out at the endless ocean. "Just think, Joey," said the father, "the waves breaking at our feet came from far across the sea."

After a few minutes of contemplation, Joey observed sadly, "The waves are dying at our feet. They came to the end of their long trip from across the ocean and then they die. This is the end for the waves."

"No," the father replied, "this is not the end. This is the beginning – the beginning of their long journey back across the sea."

And so, as we come to the end of this book, we realize – as Joey's father said, that this is not really the end. This is the beginning of your quest for a stronger, happier family – not only for your family, but for your children and for your children's children. And for generations to come, the ripple effect of your efforts today will extend far into the future.

May God bless you as you build a strong family!

APPENDIX A
ASSESSING YOUR FAMILY'S STRENGTHS

You and your family may enjoy responding to this instrument. It is a tool to guide you in becoming more aware of the strengths that exist in your family and the areas in which you would like to grow.

The qualities of strong families can be broken down into six general categories, as outlined below. Put an "S," for *strength*, beside the qualities you feel your family has achieved. These will serve as the foundation for your family's growth and positive change together.

Put a "G," for *growth*, beside those qualities that are areas of potential growth. These are areas your family would like to work on together to improve. If the particular characteristic does not apply to your family or is not a characteristic important to you, put an "NA," for *not applicable*.

COMMITMENT
1.____ We are "always there" for each other.
2.____ We are dedicated to our marriage as the core of the family.
3.____ We (spouses) are faithful to each other sexually.
4.____ We value each family member as a precious part of the family.
5.____ We take care of each other and help each other.
6.____ We share many family goals.
7.____ We give family priority over outside activities, including work.
8.____ We are honest with each other.
9.____ We have numerous family traditions.
10.____ We will endure/stay together as a family.
11.____ We have unconditional love for each other.
12.____ We can depend on each other.
13.____ We make sacrifices for our family.
14.____ Give an overall rating (S or G) of *commitment* in your family.

SPIRITUAL WELL-BEING

15.____ We believe that God has a purpose for our lives.

16.____ We have moral values that guide us (honesty, responsibility).

17.____ We practice virtues such as patience, forgiveness, and controlling anger.

18.____ We have inner peace even in difficult times because of our relationship with God.

19.____ We have an outlook on life that is usually hopeful and confident.

20.____ We believe that God watches over and guides our family.

21.____ We are part of a spiritual family and attend worship services.

22.____ We have family and friends who share our spiritual beliefs.

23.____ We spend time each day in prayer or meditation.

24.____ We read inspirational literature.

25.____ We apply our spiritual values to everyday life.

26.____ We avoid extreme or ongoing arguments over beliefs.

27.____ Give an overall rating (S or G) of *spiritual well-being* in your family.

ABILITY TO COPE WITH STRESS AND CRISES

28.____ We are able to ignore petty irritants and minor stresses.

29.____ We don't give lots of attention or energy to worry.

30.____ We believe that daily struggles/challenges are just a part of reaching a bigger goal.

31.____ We use humor to relieve stress and tension.

32.____ We take life one day at a time.

33.____ We eliminate some involvements when our schedules get too full.

34.____ We give attention/energy to the most important things first.

35.____ We engage in recreational activities and hobbies.

36.____ We enjoy outdoor relaxation and recreation.

37.____ We participate in regular exercise.

38.____ We manage to see some good in bad situations.

39.____ We work together to face the challenges of crises.

40.____ We support each other emotionally in crises situations.

41.____ We seek help from friends, church, and neighbors during crises.

42.____ We seek professional help in crises situations.

43.____ We call on spiritual resources (God's help, faith, hope) in times of crises.

44.____ We see opportunities for personal and family growth in crises situations.

45.____ We use good communication to share feelings and to solve problems.

46.____ We are flexible and adaptable.

47.____ Give an overall rating (S or G) of _coping ability with stress and crises_ in your family.

POSITIVE COMMUNICATION AND CONFLICT RESOLUTION

48.____ We allow time for communication (conversations, discussions)

49.____ We have positive communication.

50.____ We listen to each other.

51.____ We check the meaning of messages (give feedback, seek clarification).

52.____ We see things from each other's point of view (have empathy); We are responsive to each other's concerns.

53.____ We avoid criticizing, judging, or acting superior.

54.____ We are honest and truthful (and kind).

55.____ We deal with disagreements promptly.

56.____ We deal with conflict issues one at a time.

57.____ We seek compromise or consensus in resolving conflict (rather than "win or lose").

58.____ We are specific when dealing with conflict issues.

59.____ We avoid actions and words that would be emotionally devastating to each other (blaming, name-calling, personal attacks).

60.____ We seek to understand and accept our differences.

61.____ We focus our energies on how we can best solve the problem when we experience conflict.

62.____ Give an overall rating (S or G) of _positive communication and conflict resolution_ in your family.

APPRECIATION AND AFFECTION

63.____ We show appreciation to each other every day.

64.____ We feel deep and genuine affection for each other.

65.____ We avoid criticizing each other.

66.____ We speak positively to each other.

67.____ We recognize each other's accomplishments.

68.____ We see each other's good qualities.

69.____ We look for the good in each other (dig for diamonds).

70.____ We are sincere in expressions of appreciation.

71.____ We practice good manners at home and with others.

72.____ We refrain from sarcasm and put-downs.

73.____ We cultivate humor that is gentle and positive. (No one is embarrassed or hurt by it.)

74.____ We accept compliments and kindnesses graciously.

75.____ We create a pleasant environment at home.

76.____ We feel secure and safe in our interactions with each other.

77.____ We enhance each other's self-esteem.

78.____ Give an overall rating (S or G) of _appreciation and affection_ in your family.

TIME TOGETHER

79.____ We eat meals together regularly.

80.____ We do house and yard chores together.

81.____ We spend time together in recreation (play).

82.____ We participate in religious, school, or social activities together.

83.____ We celebrate holidays, birthdays, and anniversaries as a family.

84.____ We have a family vacation.

85.____ We enjoy each other's company.

86.____ We have good times together that are unplanned and spontaneous.

87.____ We take time to be with each other.

88.____ We spend good quality time together.

89.____ Give an overall rating (S or G) of _time together_ in your family.

APPENDIX B
FAMILY STRENGTHS ACTION PLAN

It may be helpful for you to develop a Family Strengths Action Plan revolving around the six characteristics of strong families. Your action plan can be an important aid in helping your family to grow stronger – to make your dreams for your family a reality.

Family Strength: Commitment

What we want to happen:_____

_____

_____

How we are going to do it (specific strategies):_____

_____

_____

Specific time we will start:_____

Family Strength: Spiritual Well-Being

What we want to happen: _____

_____

_____

How we are going to do it (specific strategies):_____

_____

_____

Specific time we will start:_____

Family Strength: Coping Ability for Stress and Crises

What we want to happen:_____

_____

_____

How we are going to do it (specific strategies):_____

_____

_____

Specific time we will start:_____

Family Strength: Positive Communication and Conflict Resolution

What we want to happen:_____

_____

_____

How we are going to do it (specific strategies):_____

_____

_____

Specific time we will start:_____

Family Strength: Appreciation and Affection

What we want to happen:_____

_____

_____

How we are going to do it (specific strategies):_____

_____

_____

Specific time we will start:_____

Family Strength: Time Together

What we want to happen:_____

_____

_____

How we are going to do it (specific strategies):_____

_____

_____

Specific time we will start:_____

_____